.meals in
minutes

Published in 2013 by ACP Books, Sydney
ACP Books are published by ACP Magazines Limited
a division of Nine Entertainment Co.

ACP Books
Publishing Director, ACP Magazines Gerry Reynolds
Publisher Sally Wright
Editorial & food director Pamela Clark
Creative director Hieu Chi Nguyen
Art director & designer Hannah Blackmore
Senior editors Stephanie Kistner; Wendy Bryant
Food editor & nutritional information Emma Braz
Junior writer Rosie Fittler
Sales & rights director Brian Cearnes
Marketing manager Bridget Cody
Senior business analyst Rebecca Varela
Operations manager David Scotto
Production manager Corinne Whitsun-Jones
Circulation manager Nicole Pearson
Demand forecast analyst Rebecca Williams

Published by ACP Books,
a division of ACP Magazines Ltd,
54 Park St, Sydney; GPO Box 4088,
Sydney, NSW 2001.
phone (02) 9282 8618; fax (02) 9267 9438.
acpbooks@acpmagazines.com.au;
www.acpbooks.com.au

Recipe development Elizabeth Macri, Adam Cremona, Angela Portela, Lara Reynolds, Lucy Nunes, Alex Elliot
Photographer William Meppem
Stylist Vivien Walsh
Food preparation Adam Cremona, Dominic Smith
Cover Pork and rosemary meatballs with pasta, page 106

Printed by C&C Offset Printing, China.
Australia Distributed by Network Services,
phone +61 2 9282 8777; fax +61 2 9264 3278;
networkweb@networkservicescompany.com.au
www.acpbooks.com.au
New Zealand Distributed by Southern Publishers Group,
phone (9) 360 0692; fax (9) 360 0695; hub@spg.co.nz
South Africa Distributed by PSD Promotions,
phone (27 11) 392 6065/6/7; fax (27 11) 392 6079/80;
orders@psdprom.co.za

Title: Meals in minutes
Author: Pamela Clark.
ISBN: 978-174245-359-0 (pbk.)
Notes: Includes index.
Subjects: Quick and easy cooking.
Dewey Number: 641.555

© ACP Magazines Ltd 2013
ABN 18 053 273 546
This publication is copyright. No part of it may be reproduced or transmitted in any form without the written permission of the publishers.
The publishers would like to thank Sonoma – Artisan Sourdough Bakers www.sonoma.com.au

To order books
phone 136 116 (within Australia) or
order online at www.acpbooks.com.au
Send recipe enquiries to:
recipeenquiries@acpmagazines.com.au

THE AUSTRALIAN
Women's Weekly

.meals in
minutes

acp books

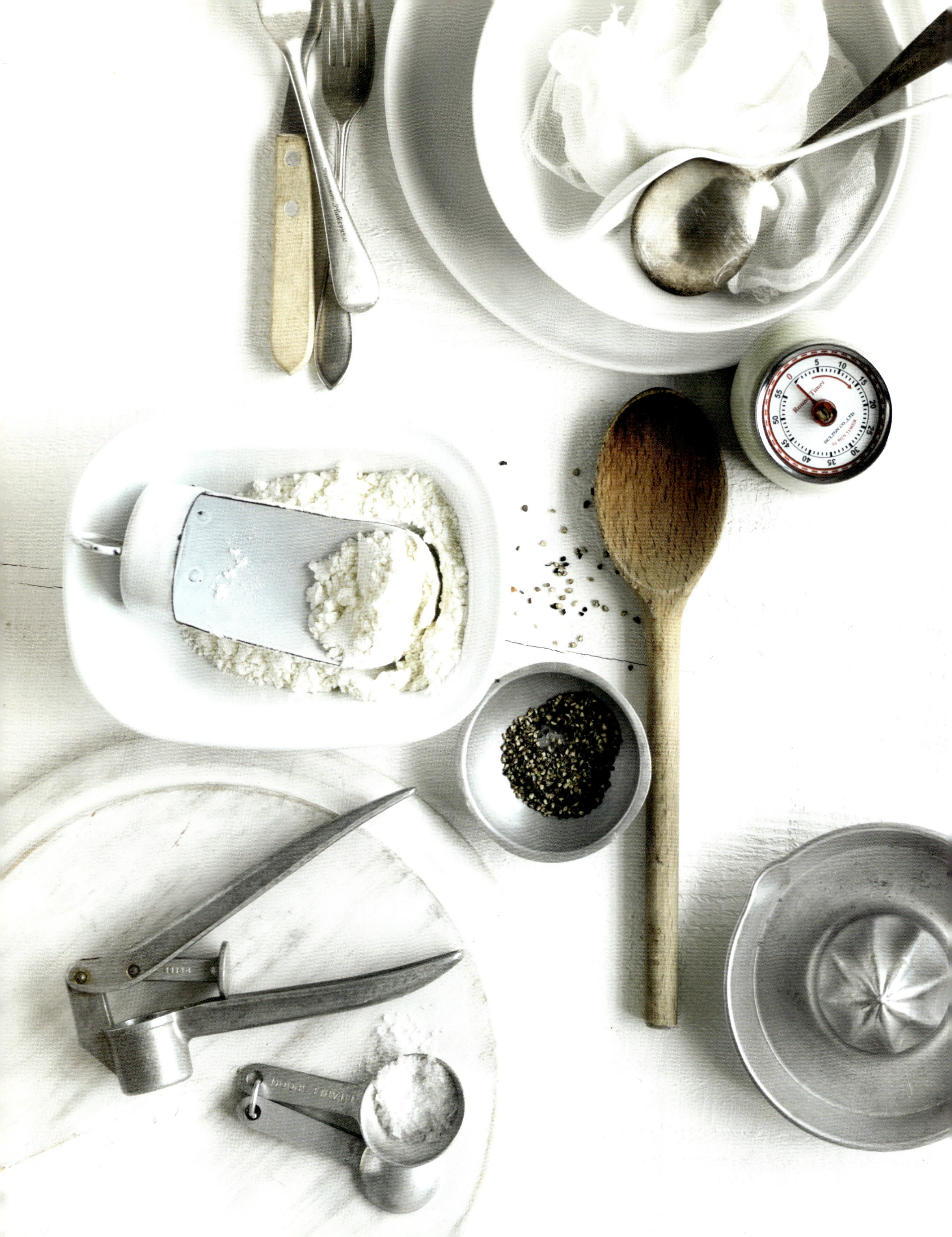

contents

kitchen express	6
poultry	8
lamb	44
beef & veal	72
pork	104
seafood	138
vegetarian	176
sides	204
glossary	234
conversion chart	237
index	238

Kitchen Express

Today, we are always busy and pushed for time, and sometimes even the thought of cooking a meal can be exhausting. As a result, we have developed a cookbook that will allow you to get a simple, fresh and fabulous meal on the table in mainly 30 minutes or less. This book will not only provide you with speedy recipes for chicken, lamb, beef, pork, seafood and vegetarian dishes, it will also inspire you, so you no longer cook the same thing time and time again. Every recipe has been tested at least three times to make sure the timing is spot on.

Before you start

The most important thing to do when 'fast' cooking is to read the entire recipe before you start. This way you know exactly how the recipe is going to flow. Once you have done this, it is time to get your equipment organised before you begin chopping and cutting. An organised kitchen is a must when cooking an entire meal in less than 30 minutes. Some of our favourite tools include a V-slicer or, mandoline, blender, food processor, good sharp knives, scissors, a sharp vegetable peeler and a really sharp grater. To ensure we cook efficiently, we have all our most commonly-used utensils within easy reach. Implementing a good system in your kitchen will make it much easier to work more quickly and multi-task. Too much clutter will reduce the amount of bench space available, slow you down and cause chaos in the kitchen.

Once your kitchen is organised, you are ready to start preparing all the ingredients (mise en place). Slice, chop, wash and measure everything before you begin.

Store-bought products

Today, there is a great range of products available at supermarkets to help speed up the cooking process. Don't be fooled by past stories of flavourless pre-made products. The selection available today has improved greatly over the past few years, and products such as pre-made sauces, curries and pastries are now great to use for all your midweek meals.

Supermarkets are not just a source of useful pre-made products, they are even removing the slicing and dicing time for you. Now you can buy peeled and chopped vegetables, mixed salad leaves, marinated and diced meats, seasoned roasts and, of course, barbecued chickens to help make your life easier.

Now you're ready to cook

While you may be pressed for time when you first start, the more you cook, the faster you will become at cooking the recipes in this book. *Meals in Minutes* will become the cookbook you use every day of the week. This collection of recipes is all about helping you prepare a meal that is fresh, delicious and fast, and that your family and friends will love.

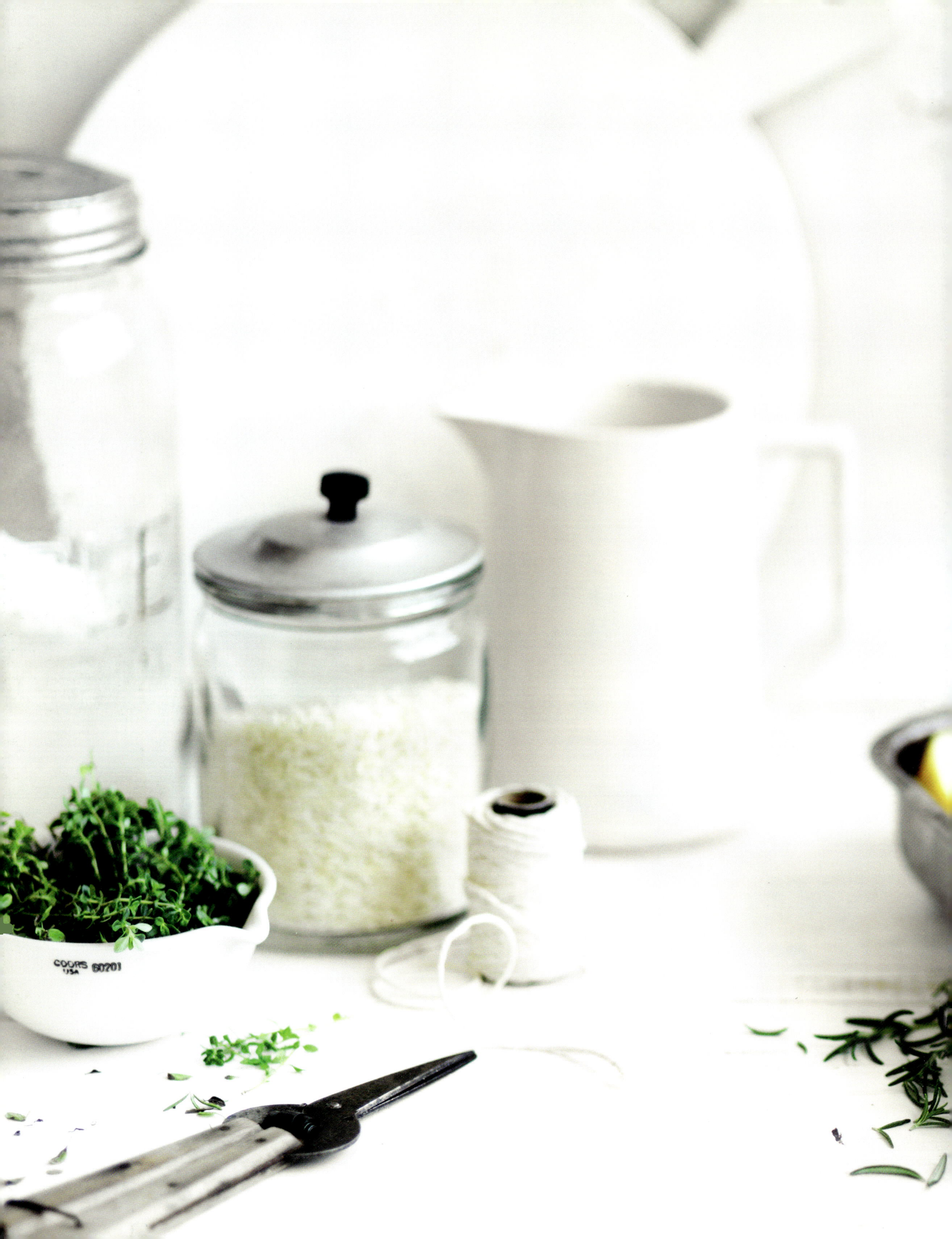
COORS USA 60201

poultry

A versatile meat that is suited to various cooking methods, poultry is often cheaper than other meat, but is full of flavour.

vietnamese chicken and mango salad

2 x 200g (6½-ounce) chicken breast fillets

2 cloves garlic, crushed

1 tablespoon coarsely chopped coriander (cilantro)

2 fresh small thai red (serrano) chillies, chopped finely

1 tablespoon oyster sauce

2 medium mangoes (860g)

2 green onions (scallions), sliced thinly

120g (4 ounces) packet salad mix leaves with cabbage and kale

1 cup loosely packed coriander leaves (cilantro), extra

1 cup loosely packed mint leaves

½ cup loosely packed vietnamese mint leaves

¼ cup (60ml) vietnamese salad dressing

1 Cut chicken in half horizontally; place in a medium bowl with garlic, chopped coriander, half the chopped chilli, and the sauce; mix well.
2 Cook chicken on a heated oiled grill plate (or grill or barbecue), about 10 minutes or until cooked through. Cool; then slice chicken thinly.
3 Meanwhile, thinly slice mangoes. Combine mango, onion, salad leaves, herbs and dressing in a large bowl. Add chicken; toss gently to combine. Season to taste.

prep + cook time 30 minutes **serves** 4
nutritional count per serving 2.3g total fat (0.6g saturated fat); 818kJ (195 cal); 16g carbohydrate; 25.3g protein; 4.1g fibre

tip You can use 120g (4 ounces) of your favourite salad leaves for this recipe.

READY IN
30
MINUTES

chicken satay skewers with crunchy salad

800g (1½ pounds) chicken thigh fillets

2 green onions (scallions), sliced finely

1 stalk celery (150g), trimmed, sliced finely

180g (5½ ounces) baby salad mix

1 cup (80g) bean sprouts

¼ cup (35g) roasted peanuts

100g (3 ounces) packaged fried noodles

¼ cup loosely packed coriander (cilantro) leaves

satay sauce

½ cup (75g) roasted peanuts, chopped coarsely

1 tablespoon light brown sugar

1 cup (250ml) coconut milk

1 teaspoon fish sauce

2 tablespoons soy sauce

1 teaspoon chilli flakes

1 tablespoon peanut butter

chilli lime dressing

1 fresh small red thai (serrano) chilli, sliced finely

¼ cup (60ml) lime juice

1 tablespoon soy sauce

1 tablespoon peanut oil

1 Make satay sauce. Reserve 1 cup of the sauce.
2 Cut chicken in half crossways. Thread onto eight 23cm (9¼-inch) metal skewers, coat with remaining satay sauce.
3 Cook skewers on a heated oiled grill plate (or grill or barbecue) about 10 minutes or until cooked through.
4 Meanwhile, make chilli lime dressing.
5 Place onion and celery in a large bowl with remaining ingredients and the dressing; toss to combine. Season to taste.
6 Serve salad with skewers and reserved satay sauce for dipping.
satay sauce Stir ingredients in a medium bowl until combined.
chilli lime dressing Place ingredients in a screw-top jar; shake well to combine.

prep + cook time 30 minutes **serves** 4
nutritional count per serving 45.7g total fat (16.3g saturated fat); 3190kJ (762 cal); 31.3g carbohydrate; 53.6g protein; 6.5g fibre

tip If using bamboo skewers, wrap the ends in foil to prevent them from burning.

READY IN 30 MINUTES

crisp parmesan chicken with eggplant salad

4 chicken breast fillets (680g)

2 eggs, beaten lightly

1½ cups (110g) panko (japanese) breadcrumbs

½ cup (40g) finely grated parmesan cheese

olive oil, for shallow-frying

8 slices char-grilled eggplant (500g), sliced thickly lengthways

2 medium tomatoes (380g), chopped coarsely

1 shallot (25g), sliced thinly

⅓ cup small basil leaves

1 tablespoon black olive tapenade

1½ tablespoons olive oil, extra

1 Cut each breast in half horizontally to make two fillets. Dip chicken in egg, then in combined breadcrumb and parmesan mixture to coat.
2 Heat enough oil in a large frying pan to come 2cm (¾-inch) up side of pan; cook chicken, in batches, over medium heat, until cooked through. Drain on absorbent paper.
3 Meanwhile, place eggplant, tomato, shallot and basil in a medium bowl; toss gently to combine. Season to taste.
4 Divide salad among serving plates; drizzle with combined tapenade and extra oil. Top with chicken.

prep + cook time 30 minutes **serves** 4
nutritional count per serving 43.4g total fat (12.3g saturated fat); 3027kJ (723 cal); 24.1g carbohydrate; 55g protein; 2.6g fibre

tip Panko breadcrumbs can be found in the Asian section of the major supermarkets.

jerk chicken with pumpkin and onion

600g (1¼ pounds) pumpkin, unpeeled, cut into thin wedges

1 large red onion (300g), cut into thin wedges

¼ cup (60ml) olive oil

2 green onions (scallions), chopped coarsely

2 cloves garlic, quartered

1 teaspoon each cracked black pepper, ground allspice and dried chilli flakes

1½ tablespoons fresh thyme leaves

1½ tablespoons honey

6 chicken thigh fillets (660g)

¼ cup fresh coriander leaves (cilantro)

1 Preheat oven to 220°C/425°F. Place pumpkin and red onion, in a single layer, on a baking-paper-lined oven tray. Drizzle with 1 tablespoon of the oil. Season. Bake for about 20 minutes or until tender.
2 Meanwhile, blend or process green onion, garlic, spices, thyme, honey and remaining oil until smooth.
3 Halve chicken crossways. Cook chicken on heated oiled grill plate (or grill or barbecue), brushing with honey mixture, until cooked through.
4 Place pumpkin and red onion on serving plates. Top with chicken; season to taste, sprinkle over coriander leaves. Serve with remaining honey mixture, if you like.

prep + cook time 30 minutes **serves** 4
nutritional count per serving 22.7g total fat (4.7g saturated fat); 1850kJ (442 cal); 22.6g carbohydrate; 34.2g protein; 6.8g fibre

tip Accompany chicken with a Greek-style yoghurt, if you like.

crisp parmesan chicken with eggplant salad

jerk chicken with pumpkin and onion

poultry 15

steamed orange ginger chicken with greens

4 baby buk choy (600g), halved

500g (1 pound) choy sum, trimmed, cut into 6cm (2½-inch) lengths

4 chicken breast fillets (680g)

4cm (1½-inch) piece fresh ginger (20g), peeled

1 tablespoon pink peppercorns, crushed

2 tablespoons coarsely grated orange rind

1 teaspoon sesame oil

2 green onions (scallions), sliced thinly

soy sesame dressing

1 tablespoon salt-reduced soy sauce

1 tablespoon rice vinegar

1 tablespoon peanut oil

1 teaspoon sesame oil

1½ tablespoons orange juice

1 Place buk choy and choy sum over base of a large bamboo steamer. Cut chicken diagonally crossways into three pieces; place on vegetables.
2 Cut ginger lengthways into thin strips, cut into matchstick-sized pieces. Sprinkle ginger, peppercorns, rind and oil over chicken. Season. Steam chicken, covered, over wok or large frying pan of simmering water about for 10 minutes or until cooked through.
3 Meanwhile, make soy sesame dressing.
4 Serve chicken and vegetables, drizzled with dressing and onion.
soy sesame dressing Whisk ingredients in a small jug until combined.

prep + cook time 30 minutes **serves** 4
nutritional count per serving 10.3g total fat (2g saturated fat); 1290kJ (308 cal); 4.3g carbohydrate; 45.3g protein; 7.8g fibre

tip Use a zester to get long thin strips of orange rind.
serving suggestion Steamed jasmine rice.

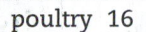

READY IN
30 MINUTES

READY IN
30
MINUTES

duck breasts with roasted vegetables

READY IN
20
MINUTES

thai chicken, papaya and peanut salad

duck breasts with roasted vegetables

400g (12½ ounces) baby carrots, trimmed

1 large red onion (300g), sliced thickly

170g (5½ ounces) asparagus, trimmed

2 teaspoons olive oil

4 x 150g (4½-ounce) duck breast fillets, skin on

¼ cup (90g) plum sauce

1 tablespoon sweet chilli sauce

200g (6½ ounces) baby vine-ripened truss tomatoes

1 Preheat oven to 180°C/350°F.
2 Combine carrots, onion, asparagus and oil on a large baking tray; season. Roast about 15 minutes or until vegetables are tender.
3 Meanwhile, place duck, skin-side down, in a large frying pan; cook, over medium heat, turning occasionally, until browned. Transfer to a large baking tray lined with baking paper.
4 Combine sauces in a small jug. Brush both sides of duck with sauce mixture; add tomatoes to baking tray. Roast duck and tomatoes for about 5 minutes or until tomatoes soften.
5 Serve duck and tomatoes with roasted vegetables.

prep + cook time 30 minutes **serves** 4
nutritional count per serving 14.5g total fat (4.1g saturated fat); 1706kJ (407 cal); 24.8g carbohydrate; 41.3g protein; 6.8g fibre

tip Place the duck breast skin-side down in a cold frying pan, then turn on the heat; this helps render off some of the fat.

thai chicken, papaya and peanut salad

½ barbecued chicken (500g)

½ small green papaya (325g), grated coarsely

½ cup (75g) roasted peanuts, chopped coarsely

250g (8 ounces) shredded vegetable salad mix

75g (2½ ounces) baby salad mix

1 cup fresh coriander leaves (cilantro)

½ cup (125ml) asian-style salad dressing

1 Remove meat from chicken, discarding skin and bones. Coarsely chop chicken.
2 Place chicken and papaya in a large bowl with peanuts, salad mixes, coriander and dressing; toss gently to combine. Season to taste.

prep time 20 minutes **serves** 4
nutritional count per serving 12g total fat (2.2g saturated fat); 1167kJ (279 cal); 14.8g carbohydrate; 25.2g protein; 5.9g fibre

tip Shredded vegetable salad mix contains carrot, beetroot and broccoli stem. It is found in the chilled lettuce section of major supermarkets. You could use coarsely grated vegetables if salad mix is unavailable.

READY IN
25
MINUTES

tips Dried cranberries are sometimes labelled 'craisins' and can be found in the baking aisle of supermarkets. Chicken breast fillets can be substituted for turkey, if you like. Coriander is one of the few fresh herbs to be sold with its root attached. It should be readily available from greengrocers. Asian greengrocers will certainly stock it.

turkey pilaf

1 sprig fresh coriander (cilantro) with root attached

1 tablespoon olive oil

600g (1¼ pounds) turkey breast fillets, sliced thinly

1 medium brown onion (150g), sliced thinly

1 clove garlic, sliced thinly

1 cinnamon stick

1 teaspoon yellow mustard seeds

1½ cups (300g) basmati rice

1½ cups (375ml) water

1½ cups (375ml) chicken stock

⅓ cup (45g) dried cranberries

¼ cup (35g) roasted unsalted shelled pistachios, chopped coarsely

½ cup coriander leaves (cilantro), extra

1 Remove leaves from the coriander stem and reserve. Finely chop the coriander root and stem.

2 Heat oil in a large saucepan; cook turkey, in batches, over medium heat until browned. Remove from pan.

3 Cook onion in same pan, stirring, until softened. Add garlic, coriander root and stem, cinnamon and mustard seeds; cook, stirring, until fragrant. Stir in rice, the water and stock; bring to the boil. Reduce heat; cook, covered, over low heat, about 10 minutes or until rice is tender.

4 Stir turkey and cranberries into pilaf; cook 5 minutes. Season to taste. Cover; stand 5 minutes.

5 Serve pilaf sprinkled with nuts and both the reserved and extra coriander leaves.

prep + cook time 25 minutes **serves** 4
nutritional count per serving 10g total fat (1.4g saturated fat); 2335kJ (558 cal); 69.9g carbohydrate; 43.8g protein; 3.5g fibre

chermoulla barbecued chicken thighs

2 cloves garlic

2 shallots (50g)

1 fresh small red thai (serrano) chilli

1 sprig fresh coriander (cilantro) with root attached

2 teaspoons ground cumin

1 teaspoon smoked paprika

1 tablespoon olive oil

8 x 125g (4-ounce) chicken thigh fillets

2 medium lemons (280g), halved

pea puree

500g (1 pound) frozen baby peas

25g (¾ ounce) butter

2 tablespoons water

300g (9½ ounces) sour cream

1 Blend or process garlic, shallots, chilli, coriander, spices and oil until almost smooth. Place in a large bowl with chicken; rub to coat chicken all over.
2 Cook chicken and lemons on heated, oiled grill plate (or grill or barbecue), until chicken is cooked. Using tongs, squeeze grilled lemon over chicken.
3 Meanwhile, make pea puree.
4 Serve chicken with pea puree.
pea puree Stir peas, butter and water in a medium saucepan, over medium heat, for about 5 minutes or until peas are tender and butter is melted. Blend or process pea mixture with sour cream until smooth.

prep + cook time 30 minutes **serves** 4
nutritional count per serving 32.6g total fat (14g saturated fat); 2534kJ (605 cal); 15.2g carbohydrate; 58g protein; 10.4g fibre

serving suggestion Baby rocket leaves.

chicken breasts with walnut pesto

1 tablespoon olive oil

4 x 200g (6½-ounce) chicken breast fillets

2 cloves garlic

1 cup (100g) roasted walnuts

1½ cups firmly packed fresh mint leaves

1½ cups firmly packed fresh parsley leaves

¼ cup (60ml) lemon juice

½ cup (125ml) olive oil, extra

1 tablespoon torn fresh flat-leaf parsley leaves

1 lemon, cut into wedges

1 Preheat oven to 180°C/350°F.
2 Heat oil in a large frying pan on stove top; cook chicken, over medium heat, until browned both sides. Place chicken on a large baking tray; transfer to oven. Cook, uncovered, about 10 minutes or until chicken is cooked through.
3 Meanwhile, blend or process garlic, walnuts, herbs and juice until finely chopped. While motor is operating, add extra oil in a thin steady steam; blend until mixture is combined. Season.
4 Serve chicken topped with walnut pesto and torn parsley; accompany with lemon wedges.

prep + cook time 20 minutes **serves** 4
nutritional count per serving 53.8g total fat (7.4g saturated fat); 2919kJ (697 cal); 2.2g carbohydrate; 49.9g protein; 5.3g fibre

serving suggestion Potato puree (page 216) and steamed green beans.

chermoulla barbecued chicken thighs

chicken breasts with walnut pesto

READY IN
40
MINUTES

tip Chorizo is a sausage made of coarsely ground pork and highly seasoned with garlic and chilli. It is available both smoked and dry-cured, or fresh (raw). It's widely used in Spanish, Portuguese and Mexican cookery, although each country has its own variation. It is available from the delicatessen section of some supermarkets, as well as Spanish delicatessens and some speciality butcher shops.

spanish chicken and chorizo stew

1 cup (250ml) chicken stock

pinch saffron threads

340g (11 ounces) cured chorizo sausage, sliced thickly

1.5kg (3 pounds) chicken drumsticks

2 teaspoons olive oil

1 medium brown onion (150g), sliced thickly

1 medium red capsicum (bell pepper) (200g), sliced thickly

2 teaspoons smoked paprika

800g (1½ pounds) canned crushed tomatoes

½ cup (75g) seeded black olives

¼ cup fresh flat-leaf parsley leaves

1 Combine stock and saffron in a small bowl. Set aside until required.
2 Cook chorizo in a large saucepan, over medium heat, until browned. Drain on absorbent paper.
3 Cook chicken, in batches, in the same pan, until browned all over. Remove from pan.
4 Heat oil in the same pan, add onion and capsicum; cook, stirring, about 2 minutes or until onion softens. Add paprika; cook, stirring, until fragrant.
5 Return chorizo and chicken to pan. Add stock mixture and tomatoes, cover; bring to the boil. Reduce heat; simmer, covered, about 20 minutes or until chicken is cooked through. Stir in olives.
6 Serve stew sprinkled with parsley; accompany with crusty bread rolls, if you like.

prep + cook time 40 minutes **serves** 6
nutritional count per serving 29.7g total fat (8.7g saturated fat); 1970kJ (470 cal); 8g carbohydrate; 41.1g protein; 4.3g fibre

moroccan-spiced chicken casserole

1.3kg (2¾ pounds) chicken thigh fillets

1 tablespoon moroccan spice mix

2 tablespoons olive oil

400g (12½ ounces) canned chickpeas (garbanzo beans), rinsed, drained

½ cup (75g) dried apricots

1 large brown onion (200g), sliced thinly

800g (1½ pounds) canned crushed tomatoes

½ cup (125ml) chicken stock

1 Preheat oven to 200°C/400°F.
2 Place chicken and spice mix in a large bowl; rub to coat.
3 Heat half the oil in a large frying pan; cook chicken, in batches, until browned both sides. Transfer chicken to a 4-litre (16-cup) ovenproof dish. Add chickpeas and apricots.
4 Heat remaining oil in same frying pan; cook onion, stirring, until softened. Add tomatoes and stock to pan; bring to the boil. Carefully pour tomato mixture over chicken mixture; cover. Transfer to oven; roast about 15 minutes or until chicken is cooked through. Season to taste.

prep + cook time 30 minutes **serves** 4
nutritional count per serving 32.5g total fat (8.1g saturated fat); 3192kJ (763 cal); 27.3g carbohydrate; 85.7g protein; 8.6g fibre

serving suggestion Green onion couscous (page 207).

chicken thighs with burnt-orange sauce

⅔ cup (150g) caster (superfine) sugar

½ cup (125ml) water

2 teaspoons finely grated orange rind

⅓ cup (80ml) orange juice

1 tablespoon olive oil

1 tablespoon apple cider vinegar

8 x 125g (4-ounce) chicken thigh fillets

1 Stir sugar and the water in a small saucepan over medium heat until sugar dissolves. Bring to the boil; boil, without stirring, about 5 minutes or until a light golden colour. Remove from heat; allow bubbles to subside. Stir in rind, juice, oil and vinegar. (If toffee hardens, return to a low heat until melted.)
2 Meanwhile, cook chicken on a heated oiled grill plate (or grill or barbecue), until brown all over and cooked through.
3 Serve chicken drizzled with burnt-orange sauce.

prep + cook time 20 minutes **serves** 4
nutritional count per serving 26.3g total fat (7.5g saturated fat); 2635kJ (629 cal); 39.1g carbohydrate; 60.6g protein; 0.1g fibre

serving suggestion Green onion couscous (page 207).

moroccan-spiced chicken casserole

chicken thighs with burnt-orange sauce

READY IN 20 MINUTES

tip You will need about two iceberg lettuces for this recipe. To easily separate lettuce leaves without tearing, use a sharp knife to remove the core at the base of the lettuce. Hold the lettuce, cut-side up, under cold running water. Gently separate leaves one at a time, using the weight of the running water between the leaves to assist you.

chilli chicken san choy bow

1 tablespoon peanut oil

2 cloves garlic, crushed

10cm (4-inch) piece fresh ginger (50g), grated finely

4 fresh long red chillies, chopped finely

1kg (2 pounds) minced (ground) chicken

⅓ cup (80ml) oyster sauce

230g (7 ounces) canned sliced water chestnuts, rinsed, drained

2 cups (160g) bean sprouts

4 green onions (scallions), sliced thinly

12 iceberg lettuce leaves

⅓ cup (50g) roasted unsalted cashews

1 Heat oil in a large, deep frying pan; cook garlic, ginger and chilli, stirring, over high heat, 1 minute or until fragrant.
2 Add chicken to the pan; cook, stirring, until browned. Add sauce, chestnuts, sprouts and onion; stir until heated through.
3 Spoon chicken mixture into lettuce leaves; sprinkle with nuts. Accompany with lemon wedges and sliced chilli, if you like.

prep + cook time 20 minutes **serves** 6
nutritional count per serving 22.5g total fat (5.8g saturated fat); 2038kJ (487 cal); 14.2g carbohydrate; 46.9g protein; 19.6g fibre

curry lemon chicken burgers

500g (1 pound) lean minced (ground) chicken

1 tablespoon mild curry powder

2 green onions (scallions), sliced thinly

2 teaspoons finely grated lemon rind

1 egg

½ cup (140g) thick greek-style yogurt

1½ tablespoons lemon juice

2 tablespoons olive oil

4 round turkish bread rolls (660g)

80g (2½ ounces) baby rocket leaves (arugula)

1 cup (160g) drained marinated char-grilled eggplant, halved crossways

1 Combine chicken, curry powder, onion, rind and egg in a medium bowl; season.
2 Using damp hands, shape chicken mixture into four even-sized patties. Place patties on a baking-paper-lined oven tray. Cover; refrigerate 10 minutes.
3 Meanwhile, combine yogurt and juice in a small bowl. Season to taste.
4 Heat oil in a large frying pan over medium heat; cook patties, in batches, flattened slightly, about 3 minutes each side or until golden and cooked through.
5 Split bread rolls in half. Sandwich rocket, patty, eggplant and yogurt mixture between rolls.

prep + cook time 20 minutes **serves** 4
nutritional count per serving 27.4g total fat (6.7g saturated fat); 3135kJ (749 cal); 79g carbohydrate; 42.8g protein; 6.9g fibre

serving suggestion Roasted potato wedges or chips.

READY IN
20 MINUTES

READY IN
20
MINUTES

READY IN
25
MINUTES

blue cheese, apple and barbecued chicken slaw

chicken, fetta and mushroom pasta

blue cheese, apple and barbecued chicken slaw

⅓ cup (45g) flaked almonds

1 large green apple (200g), unpeeled

3 cups (480g) shredded barbecued chicken

⅓ cup roughly chopped fresh chives

500g (1 pound) packaged coleslaw mix

100g (3 ounces) blue cheese, crumbled

½ cup (125ml) coleslaw dressing

1 Place nuts in a single layer in a dry frying pan; cook over a low heat until fragrant and just changed in colour. Place in a large bowl.
2 Cut unpeeled apple into matchstick-size pieces; add to bowl with nuts. Add chicken, chives, coleslaw mix, cheese and dressing to bowl; toss gently to combine. Season to taste.
3 Serve salad with crusty bread, if you like.

prep + cook time 20 minutes **serves** 4
nutritional count per serving 26.6g total fat (7.5g saturated fat); 1907kJ (456 cal); 19.4g carbohydrate; 31.1g protein; 6.1g fibre

tips You will need a barbecued chicken weighing about 900g (1¾ pounds) for this recipe. We used gorgonzola, but any blue cheese will work well with this dish.

chicken, fetta and mushroom pasta

500g (1 pound) spiral pasta

2 tablespoons garlic butter spread

200g (6½ ounces) thinly sliced cap mushrooms

2 green onions (scallions), sliced thinly

3 cups (480g) shredded barbecued chicken

200g (6½ ounces) danish fetta cheese, crumbled

300ml (½ pint) pouring cream

2 tablespoons coarsely chopped fresh tarragon

2 green onions (scallions), extra, sliced thinly

1 Cook pasta in a large saucepan of boiling salted water until tender. Drain, reserving 2 cups of the cooking liquid. Wipe saucepan clean.
2 Melt butter in cleaned pan; cook mushrooms, over medium heat, stirring until golden and tender.
3 Return pasta to pan; add onions and chicken. Stir in cheese, cream, tarragon and reserved cooking liquid; cook, stirring until creamy and heated through. Season to taste.
4 Serve pasta topped with extra onions.

prep + cook time 25 minutes **serves** 6
nutritional count per serving 34.8g total fat (20.1g saturated fat); 2993kJ (715 cal); 60.4g carbohydrate; 37.8g protein; 3.3g fibre

tip You will need a barbecued chicken weighing about 900g (1¾ pounds) for this recipe.
serving suggestion Green bean and tomato salad with hazelnut dressing (page 232).

note Koftas are simply minced (ground) meat mixed with spices, and often onions, and rolled into balls. They are usually rolled into a round shape, although in many Arab countries they are shaped into ovals. Koftas can be cooked in many ways, including grilled, poached, fried and baked; they may be served as is, or covered in a sauce.

turkey koftas

500g (1 pound) minced (ground) turkey

1 small red onion (100g), chopped finely

1/3 cup (35g) packaged breadcrumbs

2 tablespoons finely chopped fresh coriander (cilantro) stems, reserve leaves

2 teaspoons minced ginger

1 tablespoon peanut oil

1 cup (300g) mild satay sauce

1½ cups (375ml) canned coconut cream

2/3 cup firmly packed fresh coriander leaves (cilantro)

2 medium bananas (400g), sliced thinly

1/3 cup (25g) desiccated coconut

¼ cup (35g) whole roasted unsalted peanuts

4 naan breads (280g)

1 Combine turkey, onion, breadcrumbs, coriander stems and ginger in a large bowl. Season.
2 With damp hands, roll the turkey mixture into 12 x 7cm (2¾-inch) sausage shapes. Place kofta on a baking-paper-lined baking tray. Cover; refrigerate 10 minutes.
3 Heat oil in a deep, large frying pan; cook koftas, over medium heat, until browned all over.
4 Add sauce and coconut cream to same pan; bring to the boil. Reduce heat; simmer, uncovered, about 8 minutes or until sauce thickens slightly. Add koftas and half the coriander leaves. Reduce heat; simmer, covered, about 5 minutes or until koftas are cooked through.
5 Meanwhile, toss banana and coconut in a medium bowl.
6 Serve koftas topped with peanuts and remaining coriander. Serve with coconut banana and naan bread.

prep + cook time 20 minutes **serves** 4
nutritional count per serving 59.4g total fat (29.1g saturated fat); 4245kJ (1014 cal); 74.3g carbohydrate; 43.1g protein; 9.7g fibre

READY IN 20 MINUTES

READY IN
30
MINUTES

tips Cook 1 cup (200g) basmati rice if you are unable to buy microwave rice. Chicken wing nibbles are also known as chicken wingettes.

peri peri coconut chicken curry

1 tablespoon olive oil

1.5kg (3 pounds) chicken wing nibbles

1 medium brown onion (150g), chopped coarsely

⅓ cup (80ml) sweet sherry

750g (1½ pounds) bottled coconut curry with peri peri cooking sauce

1 cup (250ml) water

⅔ cup (70g) frozen sliced beans

⅓ cup (25g) shredded coconut

500g (1 pound) packaged basmati microwave rice

1 Heat oil in a large heavy-based saucepan; cook chicken, in batches, until browned all over.
2 Add onion and sherry; cook, stirring, until onion softens. Add sauce and the water; bring to the boil. Reduce heat; simmer, covered, for about 15 minutes. Stir in beans; simmer, covered, about 10 minutes or until chicken is tender and cooked through.
3 Meanwhile, stir coconut in a medium frying pan, over low heat, about 3 minutes or until golden. Remove coconut from the pan immediately to prevent over-browning.
4 Cook rice following instructions on packet. Place rice in a medium bowl with coconut; stir to combine.
5 Serve curry with coconut rice.

prep + cook time 30 minutes **serves** 4
nutritional count per serving 58.9g total fat (18.6g saturated fat); 3953kJ (944 cal); 52.8g carbohydrate; 45.4g protein; 2.7g fibre

chicken and potato salad

750g (1½ pounds) kipfler (fingerling) potatoes, unpeeled

1 cup (120g) frozen peas

½ barbecued chicken (450g)

3 slices prosciutto (45g)

⅓ cup (80ml) white wine vinegar

¼ cup (60ml) extra virgin olive oil

1 cup loosely packed fresh small basil leaves

½ cup loosely packed fresh mint leaves

3 green onions (scallions), sliced thinly

½ cup (75g) drained sun-dried tomatoes, halved

1 Place potatoes in a large saucepan of cold salted water; bring to the boil. Boil about 15 minutes or until tender. Add peas to pan for the last minute of cooking time. Drain. Cut potatoes in half crossways.
2 Meanwhile, discard chicken skin and bones; coarsely shred meat.
3 Heat a medium frying pan over high heat; cook prosciutto until crisp. Drain on absorbent paper.
4 Combine vinegar and oil in a serving bowl; season. Add warm potatoes and peas; toss to coat in oil mixture. Add remaining ingredients; toss gently to combine.

prep + cook time 25 minutes **serves** 4
nutritional count per serving 21.6g total fat (4.5g saturated fat); 1930kJ (461 cal); 32.4g carbohydrate; 28.4g protein; 8.8g fibre

tips You can use any firm, waxy potatoes, such as pontiac or desiree, for this salad. You will need about 1½ cups (240g) coarsely shredded cooked chicken.

READY IN
25
MINUTES

indian chicken pilaf

hoisin and lemon chicken skewers

indian chicken pilaf

400g (12½ ounces) chicken thigh fillets

1½ tablespoons ghee

1 medium brown onion (150g), chopped finely

2 cloves garlic, crushed

4cm (1½-inch) piece fresh ginger (20g), grated finely

1 cinnamon stick

2 teaspoons garam masala

1 teaspoon ground turmeric

2 cups (400g) basmati rice

3 cups (750ml) chicken stock

2 tablespoons flaked almonds

½ cup coarsely chopped fresh coriander (cilantro)

1 Trim fat from chicken; cut into bite-sized pieces.
2 Heat half the ghee in a large saucepan; cook chicken, over high heat, in batches, until browned. Remove from pan.
3 Heat remaining ghee in same pan; cook onion, stirring, until softened. Stir in garlic, ginger and spices; cook until fragrant. Stir in rice and chicken until well coated. Add stock; bring to the boil. Reduce heat to low; simmer, covered, about 13 minutes or until rice is tender, stock is absorbed and chicken is cooked through. Remove from heat; stand, covered, for 5 minutes.
4 Meanwhile, place nuts in a single layer in a dry frying pan; cook over low heat until fragrant and just changed in colour. Remove from pan immediately.
5 Serve pilaf sprinkled with coriander and nuts. Accompany with yogurt and pappadums, if you like.

prep + cook time 30 minutes **serves** 4
nutritional count per serving 16.8g total fat (6.9g saturated fat); 2517kJ (601 cal); 83g carbohydrate; 27.5g protein; 2.6g fibre

hoisin and lemon chicken skewers

800g (1½ pounds) chicken thigh fillets

⅓ cup (80ml) hoisin sauce

¼ cup (60ml) lemon juice

2 tablespoons fish sauce

3 teaspoons light brown sugar

1 Trim fat from chicken; cut into long strips. Thread chicken onto eight x 23cm (9¼-inch) skewers; place on a large plate.
2 Combine remaining ingredients in a small bowl. Pour half the marinade over chicken; turn to coat.
3 Cook chicken on a heated oiled grill plate (or grill or barbecue), turning and brushing with remaining marinade until browned all over and cooked through.
4 Accompany skewers with steamed rice, broccolini and lemon wedges, if you like.

prep + cook time 25 minutes **serves** 4
nutritional count per serving 11.1g total fat (3.2g saturated fat); 1237kJ (295 cal); 10.6g carbohydrate; 37.4g protein; 2.2g fibre

tips You can prepare the chicken the night before; store, covered, in the refrigerator. You could also use pork fillet for this recipe, if you like. If using bamboo skewers, wrap the ends in foil to prevent them from burning.

note The warm colours and flavours of Moroccan food have their origin in an assortment of wonderful spices. Including harissa, paprika, ras el hanout, ginger, cumin, cinnamon and saffron, the spices are balanced to enhance the flavour of the food, while the aroma readies the appetite for what is to come. It's important to use fresh spices that still retain their fragrant flavour and aroma.

moroccan chicken

1 tablespoon moroccan spice mix

4 chicken thigh cutlets, skin on (800g)

1 tablespoon olive oil

1 large red onion (300g), cut into wedges

1 cup (250ml) chicken stock

200g (6½ ounces) green beans, halved

1 tablespoon lemon juice

1 tablespoon finely chopped preserved lemon rind

1 Sprinkle seasoning over chicken.
2 Heat oil in a large frying pan over medium heat; cook chicken, about 5 minutes or until browned all over. Remove from pan.
3 Cook onion in same pan, stirring, about 5 minutes or until softened and browned lightly.
4 Return chicken to pan, skin-side up. Stir in stock; simmer, covered, about 10 minutes. Add beans; simmer for 5 minutes or until chicken is cooked through. Stir in juice.
5 Serve chicken sprinkled with preserved lemon rind.

prep + cook time 30 minutes **serves** 4
nutritional count per serving 30.8g total fat (8.6g saturated fat); 1683kJ (402 cal); 5.8g carbohydrate; 24.5g protein; 3.4g fibre

tip You could also use chicken thigh fillets.
serving suggestion Preserved lemon and olive couscous (page 208).

READY IN 30 MINUTES

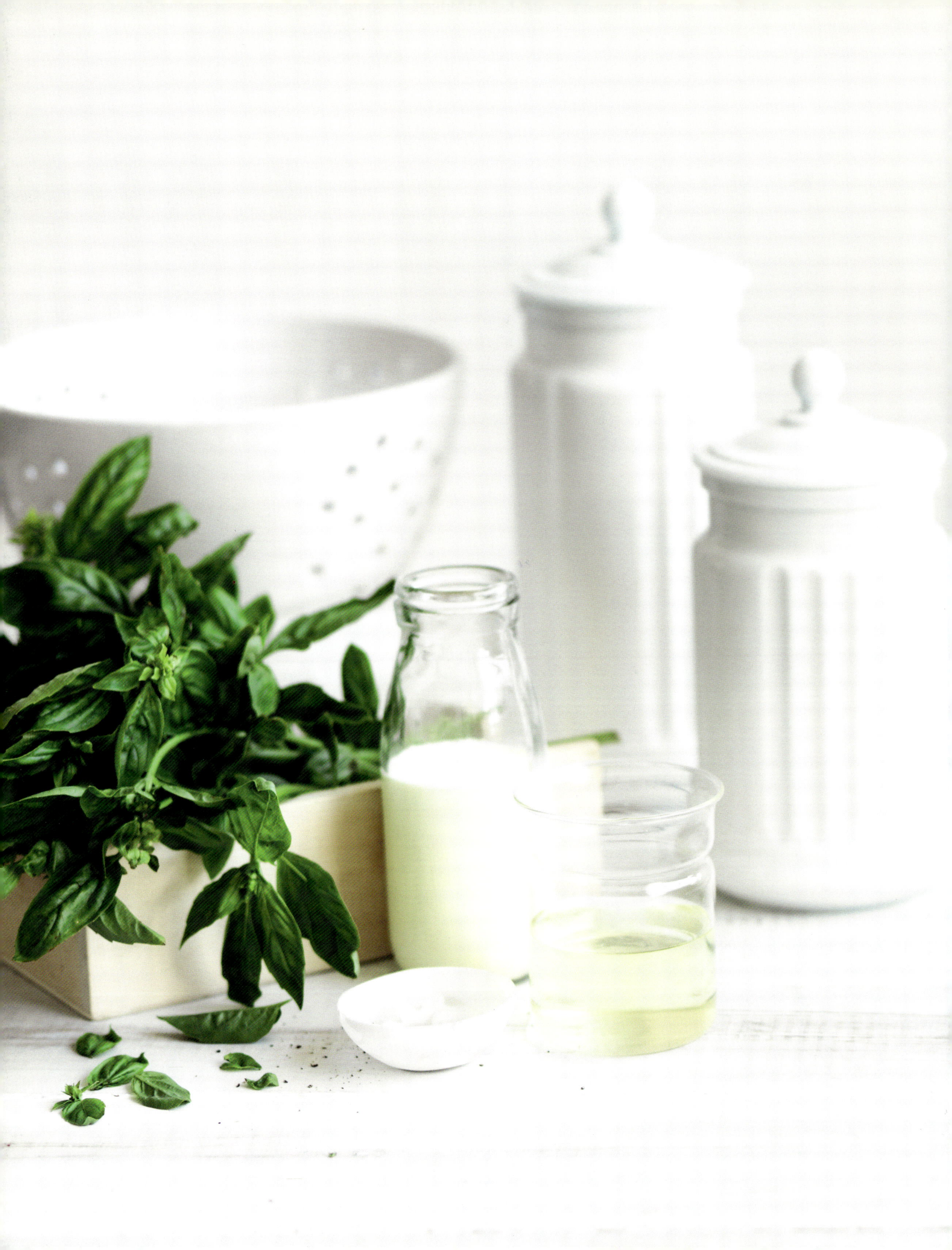

lamb

Beautiful spring lamb is a winner in any recipe, be it in a salad, as kebabs or just grilled on the barbie...perfect.

READY IN 30 MINUTES

tips Run a teaspoon down the centre of the cucumber to remove the seeds. If using bamboo skewers, cover the wooden ends with foil to prevent them from burning during cooking.

mint and honey lamb skewers with tzatziki

2 cloves garlic, quartered

½ cup loosely packed fresh mint leaves

½ teaspoon each cracked black pepper and sea salt flakes

2 tablespoons olive oil

⅓ cup (115g) honey

8 lamb fillets (550g)

tzatziki dressing

1 lebanese cucumber (130g), halved lengthways

2 tablespoons lemon juice

1 clove garlic, crushed

1 cup (280g) yogurt

1 Pound garlic, mint, pepper and salt in a mortar and pestle until mixture resembles a thick green paste. Stir in oil and 1 tablespoon of the honey.
2 Thread lamb onto eight x 25cm (10-inch) metal skewers. Place lamb in a shallow baking dish; pour over mint mixture. Turn skewers to coat in the mixture.
3 Make tzatziki dressing.
4 Cook lamb on a heated oiled grill plate (or grill or barbecue) about 10 minutes, turning occasionally, or until cooked as desired. Remove lamb from heat.
5 Just before serving, drizzle lamb with remaining honey. Serve with tzatziki dressing.
tzatziki dressing Remove and discard seeds from cucumber; coarsely grate flesh into a medium bowl. Stir in remaining ingredients until combined.

prep + cook time 30 minutes **serves** 4
nutritional count per serving 21.4g total fat (7g saturated fat); 1943kJ (464 cal); 34.5g carbohydrate; 33.9g protein; 0.9g fibre

serving suggestion Garlicky beans with pine nuts (page 225).

lamb fillet salad with green pesto dressing

8 lamb fillets (550g)

1 clove garlic, crushed

1 tablespoon olive oil

1 large zucchini (150g)

2 large egg (plum) tomatoes (180g), quartered

4 flat mushrooms (320g)

350g (11 ounces) baby rocket leaves (arugula)

2 tablespoons marinating oil from goat's cheese (below)

½ cup (100g) soft marinated goat's cheese (see tip)

green pesto dressing

½ cup (130g) baby spinach pesto

¼ cup (60ml) olive oil

1 Combine lamb, garlic and oil in a medium bowl.
2 Using a vegetable peeler or mandoline, thinly slice zucchini lengthways into ribbons.
3 Cook zucchini, tomato and mushrooms on a heated oiled grill plate (or grill or barbecue) until browned and just tender. Cover to keep warm.
4 Meanwhile, cook lamb on a heated oiled grill plate (or grill or barbecue) about 5 minutes each side or until cooked as desired. Cover; stand 5 minutes.
5 Make green pesto dressing.
6 Combine vegetables, rocket and reserved marinating oil in a large bowl. Season to taste.
7 Slice lamb. Divide vegetable mixture among serving bowls, top with lamb and crumbled cheese; drizzle with the dressing.
green pesto dressing Place ingredients in a small screw-top jar; shake well to combine.

prep + cook time 25 minutes **serves** 4
nutritional count per serving 50.9g total fat (10g saturated fat); 2224kJ (536 cal); 6.9g carbohydrate; 11.7g protein; 3.8g fibre

lamb 48

tip The oil from the marinated goat's cheese adds an extra depth of flavour to this dish. The cheese we used was marinated in a mixture of olive oil, garlic, thyme and chilli.

READY IN 25 MINUTES

READY IN
30
MINUTES

tips You can used store-bought char-grilled capsicum for this recipe, if you like. Ras el hanout is a blend of Moroccan spices; 30 or more spices can be used to make the blend, which includes cardamom, mace, nutmeg, anise, cinnamon, ginger, pepper and turmeric.

moroccan lamb cutlets with roasted capsicum couscous salad

⅓ cup (80ml) olive oil

2 teaspoons ras el hanout, plus extra for sprinkling

12 french-trimmed lamb cutlets (600g)

1 medium green capsicum (bell pepper) (200g)

1 medium yellow capsicum (bell pepper) (200g)

1 medium red capsicum (bell pepper) (200g)

1 teaspoon sea salt flakes

2 cups (500ml) water

30g (1 ounce) butter

2 cups (400g) couscous

200g (6½ ounces) hummus

1½ tablespoons finely chopped preserved lemon rind

¼ cup torn fresh flat-leaf parsley leaves

1 Preheat grill (broiler).
2 Combine half the oil, spice and lamb in a large bowl; turn lamb to coat in mixture.
3 Quarter capsicums; discard seeds and membranes. Place, skin-side up, on a lined oven tray, drizzle with remaining oil; sprinkle with salt. Roast under a hot grill about 15 minutes or until skin blisters and blackens. Cover capsicum with plastic wrap or paper for 5 minutes; peel away skin, then slice thinly.
4 Meanwhile, bring the water and butter to the boil in a medium saucepan. Stir in couscous; cover, stand 5 minutes, fluffing with a fork occasionally.
5 Spoon hummus into a small serving bowl; sprinkle with extra ras el hanout.
6 Combine couscous, capsicum, preserved lemon and parsley in a large bowl.
7 Cook lamb on a heated oiled grill plate (or grill or barbecue) about 4 minutes each side or until cooked as desired.
8 Serve lamb with couscous and spiced hummus.

prep + cook time 30 minutes **serves** 4
nutritional count per serving 50.2g total fat (15.7g saturated fat); 3898kJ (931 cal); 81g carbohydrate; 33.3g protein; 12.2g fibre

korma curry meatballs

2 tablespoons vegetable oil

1 medium brown onion (150g), cut into wedges

¼ cup (75g) korma paste

810g (1½ pounds) canned diced tomatoes

¼ cup fresh curry leaves

500g (1 pound) lean minced (ground) lamb

⅓ cup (55g) currants

3 teaspoons minced (ground) ginger

1 teaspoon coarse cooking salt (kosher salt)

750g (1½ pounds) canned tiny taters (baby new potatoes), drained

½ cup (140g) tzatziki

75g (2½ ounce) assorted ready-to-eat mini pappadums

2 tablespoons curry leaves, extra

1 Heat oil in a deep large frying pan; cook onion, stirring, until softened. Stir in paste; cook, stirring, until fragrant. Add undrained tomatoes and curry leaves; bring to the boil. Reduce heat, simmer, uncovered, 10 minutes.
2 Meanwhile, combine lamb, currants and ginger in a medium bowl; season. Using damp hands, roll mixture into 16 balls.
3 Add meatballs to sauce; cook, covered, about 5 minutes, shaking pan occasionally to coat meatballs in sauce.
4 Meanwhile, halve potatoes; add to sauce. Cook, covered, about 5 minutes or until potato is heated through and meatballs are cooked through.
5 Serve meatballs with tzatziki and pappadums; sprinkle over extra curry leaves.

prep + cook time 30 minutes **serves** 4
nutritional count per serving 36.8g total fat (10.3g saturated fat); 2579kJ (616 cal); 38.8g carbohydrate; 39.6g protein; 12g fibre

serving suggestion Steamed basmati rice.

lamb and black bean stir-fry with sambal

1 tablespoon peanut oil

500g (1 pound) lamb backstrap (eye of loin), sliced thinly

300g (9½ ounces) broccoli, cut into florets

300g (9½ ounces) green beans

⅔ cup (160ml) water

300g (9½ ounces) snow peas

½ cup (125ml) black bean sauce

6 green onions (scallions), cut into 5cm (2-inch) lengths

3 teaspoons sambal oelek

1 Heat half the oil in a wok over high heat; stir-fry lamb, in batches, until browned all over. Remove from wok.
2 Heat remaining oil in wok; stir-fry broccoli, beans and half the water until tender. Return lamb to wok with peas, sauce and the remaining water; stir-fry until peas are tender and lamb is heated through. Add onion and sambal to wok; stir-fry to combine. Season to taste.

prep + cook time 30 minutes **serves** 4
nutritional count per serving 13.5g total fat (3.5g saturated fat); 1263kJ (302 cal); 8.9g carbohydrate; 33.3g protein; 5.8g fibre

serving suggestion Steamed jasmine rice.

korma curry meatballs

lamb and black bean stir-fry with sambal

lamb 53

READY IN
30 MINUTES

tip To toast nuts, place nuts, in a single layer, in a dry small frying pan and stir over a low heat until fragrant and just changed in colour. They may also be roasted in a 160°C/325°F oven for about 8 to 10 minutes. Remove the nuts from the pan immediately to avoid burning.

cardamom lamb pilaf with cashew and coriander yogurt

400g (12½ ounces) baby carrots, unpeeled, trimmed, halved lengthways

1 tablespoon pure maple syrup

¼ cup (60ml) olive oil

400g (12½ ounces) lamb backstrap (eye of loin), cut into 2.5cm (1-inch) pieces

2 medium brown onions (300g), sliced thinly

2 cloves garlic, crushed

½ teaspoon cumin seeds

6 cardamom pods, bruised

1½ cups (300g) basmati rice

3 cups (750ml) salt-reduced chicken stock

100g (3 ounces) baby spinach leaves

cashew and coriander yogurt

½ cup (140g) greek-style yogurt

2 tablespoons coarsely chopped fresh coriander (cilantro)

2 tablespoons toasted cashew nuts, chopped finely

1 Preheat oven to 220°C/425°F.
2 Place carrots on a baking-paper-lined oven tray; drizzle with syrup and 1 tablespoon of the oil. Roast about 25 minutes or until tender.
3 Meanwhile, heat 1 tablespoon of the oil in a large saucepan over high heat; cook lamb, stirring, until browned. Remove from pan.
4 Heat remaining oil in same pan; cook onion, garlic, cumin and cardamom, stirring, about 3 minutes or until onion is soft. Add rice; stir to coat in mixture. Add stock; bring to the boil. Reduce heat; simmer, covered, about 15 minutes or until rice is tender, adding lamb and spinach to pan for the last 5 minutes of cooking time. Season to taste.
5 Meanwhile, make cashew and coriander yogurt.
6 Serve pilaf topped with carrots, and extra coriander leaves, if you like; accompany with cashew and coriander yogurt.
cashew and coriander yogurt Combine ingredients in a small bowl.

prep + cook time 30 minutes **serves** 4
nutritional count per serving 26g total fat (6.4g saturated fat); 2908kJ (695 cal); 79g carbohydrate; 32.8g protein; 7g fibre

greek lamb meatballs with tomato and mint salad

500g (1 pound) minced (ground) lamb

100g (3 ounces) fetta cheese, crumbled

2 cloves garlic, crushed

½ cup (50g) packaged breadcrumbs

1 egg

1 teaspoon dried oregano

2 teaspoons ground cumin

2 teaspoons finely grated lemon rind

1 tablespoon olive oil

tomato and mint salad

400g (12½ ounces) mixed baby tomatoes

1 lebanese cucumber (130g), peeled, chopped coarsely

½ small red onion (50g), sliced thinly

½ cup fresh mint leaves

1½ tablespoons olive oil

1½ tablespoons balsamic vinegar

1 Combine lamb, fetta, garlic, breadcrumbs, egg, oregano, cumin and rind in a large bowl. Roll level tablespoons of mixture into balls.
2 Heat the oil in a large frying pan; cook meatballs, turning occasionally, until browned all over and cooked through.
3 Meanwhile, make tomato and mint salad.
4 Serve meatballs with tomato and mint salad. Accompany with light rye bread, if you like.
tomato and mint salad Depending on their size, halve or thinly slice tomatoes. Place tomatoes in a large bowl with the remaining ingredients; toss gently to combine.

prep + cook time 30 minutes **serves** 4
nutritional count per serving 36.5g total fat (12.9g saturated fat); 2211kJ (528 cal); 12.5g carbohydrate; 36g protein; 3.2g fibre

tip Mixed baby tomatoes (tomato medley) come in a packet with a variety of different baby tomatoes; some may be larger and need slicing for this recipe.

READY IN
30
MINUTES

READY IN
20
MINUTES

tip The easiest way to remove seeds from a pomegranate is to cut it in half, then release the seeds in a large bowl of water. This way you won't get splattered with juice and the white pith will float.

grilled lamb salad

⅓ cup (100g) quince paste

1 tablespoon water

600g (1¼ pounds) lamb backstrap (eye of loin)

1 medium red onion (170g), cut into wedges

2 lebanese cucumbers (260g), seeded, cut into 3cm (1¼-inch) lengths

250g (8 ounces) haloumi cheese, crumbled

1 cup fresh coriander leaves (cilantro), torn

100g (3 ounces) mesclun

½ cup (75g) pomegranate seeds

lemon dressing

⅓ cup (80ml) extra virgin olive oil

¼ cup (60ml) lemon juice

1 Combine paste and the water in a small saucepan over medium heat; cook, stirring, until smooth and heated through.
2 Brush lamb with quince mixture. Cook lamb on a heated oiled grill plate (or grill or barbecue) about 3 minutes each side or until browned all over and cooked as desired. Cover; stand 10 minutes.
3 Make lemon dressing.
4 Combine onion, cucumber, cheese, coriander, mesclun, seeds and half the dressing in a large bowl.
5 Slice lamb thinly. Combine in a small bowl with remaining dressing; toss to coat.
6 Serve salad topped with lamb.
lemon dressing Whisk ingredients in a small jug until combined.

prep + cook time 20 minutes **serves** 4
nutritional count per serving 37.9g total fat (12.9g saturated fat); 2474kJ (591 cal); 13.1g carbohydrate; 48.2g protein; 4g fibre

lamb and eggplant pies

2 teaspoons vegetable oil

1 medium red onion (170g), chopped finely

1 clove garlic, chopped finely

500g (1 pound) minced (ground) lamb

1 medium eggplant (300g), chopped coarsely

2 teaspoons ground cumin

4 medium roma (egg) tomatoes (300g), chopped coarsely

1 tablespoon lemon juice

¼ cup (40g) pine nuts

100g (3 ounces) fetta cheese, crumbled

3 sheets fillo pastry

cooking-oil spray

1 Preheat oven to 180°C/350°F. Grease four 10cm (4-inch) wide 1-cup (250ml) ovenproof dishes; place on an oven tray.
2 Heat oil in a large deep frying pan; cook onion and garlic, stirring, until soft. Add lamb; cook, stirring, until browned. Add eggplant and cumin; cook, covered, stirring occasionally, about 5 minutes or until eggplant is soft. Stir in tomato, juice and pine nuts; remove from heat. Spoon mixture into dishes; top with cheese.
3 Place one sheet of pastry on a clean, flat surface. Spray with cooking oil; place another pastry sheet on top. Repeat with remaining pastry sheet. Cut pastry down the short side into 1cm (½-inch) wide strips. Roughly scrunch pastry strips over the top of the lamb mixture.
4 Bake pies about 10 minutes or until heated through and pastry is golden.

prep + cook time 30 minutes **serves** 4
nutritional count per serving 34g total fat (11.3g saturated fat); 2129kJ (508 cal); 13g carbohydrate; 35.7g protein; 4.6g fibre

tip Cover fillo pastry sheets with a damp tea towel to prevent it from drying out while not using.
serving suggestion Oak leaf and mixed herb salad with dijon vinaigrette (page 232). Accompany with lemon wedges and greek-style yogurt, if you like.

READY IN 30 MINUTES

lamb cutlets with pesto baby gnocchi

250g (8 ounces) baby potato gnocchi

1 tablespoon olive oil

12 french-trimmed lamb cutlets (600g)

½ cup (125ml) dry white wine

½ cup (130g) basil pesto

⅓ cup (80ml) pouring cream

¼ cup firmly packed fresh small basil leaves

1 Cook gnocchi in a large saucepan of boiling water for 1 minute or until gnocchi floats to the surface; drain.
2 Heat oil in a large frying pan over medium heat; cook lamb about 2 minutes each side or until browned and cooked as desired. Remove from pan, cover; stand 5 minutes.
3 Add wine to same pan; bring to the boil. Reduce heat; simmer until the wine has reduced by about one third. Stir in pesto and cream; simmer until sauce thickens slightly. Add gnocchi; stir until heated through. Season to taste.
4 Serve lamb with gnocchi, sprinkle with basil.

prep + cook time 25 minutes **serves** 4
nutritional count per serving 40.9g total fat (14.8g saturated fat); 2282kJ (545 cal); 21.1g carbohydrate; 19.9g protein; 2g fibre

lamb farfalle

1 medium eggplant (300g), chopped coarsely

1 large zucchini (150g), chopped coarsely

1 medium red onion (170g), sliced thickly

250g (8 ounces) cherry tomatoes, halved

2 cloves garlic, crushed

cooking-oil spray

375g (12 ounces) farfalle (bowtie) pasta

600g (1¼ pounds) lamb backstrap (eye of loin)

1 teaspoon each ground coriander and ground cumin

¼ cup (60ml) olive oil

⅓ cup (80ml) lemon juice

1 cup firmly packed fresh mint leaves

50g (1½ ounces) baby spinach leaves

⅓ cup (50g) toasted pine nuts

1 Preheat oven to 180°C/350°F.
2 Place eggplant, zucchini, onion, tomato and garlic on a large baking tray; spray with cooking oil, season. Roast about 15 minutes or until tender.
3 Meanwhile, cook pasta in a large saucepan of boiling water until tender; drain.
4 Combine lamb, spices and 1 tablespoon of the oil in a large bowl; turn to coat lamb in spices.
5 Cook lamb on a heated oiled grill plate (or grill or barbecue) about 4 minutes or until browned all over and cooked as desired. Cover; stand 5 minutes. Slice thickly.
6 Combine pasta, roasted vegetables, remaining oil, lamb and remaining ingredients in a large bowl. Season to taste.

prep + cook time 30 minutes **serves** 6
nutritional count per serving 22.4g total fat (4g saturated fat); 2254kJ (539 cal); 49.3g carbohydrate; 32g protein; 5.8g fibre

READY IN
25
MINUTES

READY IN
30
MINUTES

lamb cutlets with pesto baby gnocchi

lamb farfalle

lamb 63

turkish bread with lamb and eggplant

1 tablespoon olive oil

500g (1 pound) lean minced (ground) lamb

1 medium red onion (170g), cut into thin wedges

3 teaspoons ground cumin

1 teaspoon dried chilli flakes

1 long loaf turkish bread (450g)

150g (6½ ounces) moroccan sweet potato, sesame and pistachio dip

2 cups (200g) pizza cheese

200g (4½ ounces) char-grilled eggplant

1 Preheat oven to 200°C/400°F. Line a baking tray with foil.
2 Heat oil in a medium frying pan; cook lamb and half the onion until lamb is browned. Add spices; cook, stirring, until fragrant. Season to taste. Cool for 5 minutes.
3 Split bread in half lengthways; spread cut sides with dip. Place bread on baking tray. Sprinkle with half the cheese; top with half the eggplant. Top with lamb mixture; sprinkle with remaining cheese and remaining eggplant.
4 Transfer to oven; bake about 5 minutes or until cheese is browned lightly and bread is crispy. Top with remaining onion. Cut bread into quarters. Accompany with lamb's tongue lettuce (mâche), if you like.

prep + cook time 25 minutes **serves** 6
nutritional count per serving 30.9g total fat (10.9g saturated fat); 2467kJ (589 cal); 39.6g carbohydrate; 36.5g protein; 3.7g fibre

tip You could also use pesto or a Middle-Eastern flavoured dip.

READY IN
25
MINUTES

minty lamb burgers

spicy lamb salad

lamb 66

minty lamb burgers

500g (1 pound) minced (ground) lamb

3 cloves garlic, crushed

¼ cup finely chopped fresh mint

1 tablespoon olive oil

1 loaf long turkish bread (430g)

200g (6½ ounces) tzatziki

50g (1½ ounces) watercress leaves

450g (14½ ounces) canned sliced beetroot, drained

1 Combine lamb, garlic and mint in a large bowl, season; using damp hands, shape mixture into four even-sized patties.
2 Heat the oil in a large frying pan; cook patties for about 5 minutes each side or until browned and just cooked through.
3 Preheat grill (broiler).
4 Meanwhile, cut bread into four pieces; split each piece in half. Toast both sides under hot grill.
5 Sandwich tzatziki, watercress, beetroot and patties between bread slices.

prep + cook time 30 minutes **makes** 4
nutritional count per burger 31.2g total fat (10.2g saturated fat); 2864kJ (684 cal); 56.8g carbohydrate; 41.3g protein; 8.1g fibre

tip Patties tend to shrink when cooking, so make sure you make them about 12cm (4¾-inch) in diameter.
serving suggestion Oven-roasted fries.

spicy lamb salad

1 teaspoon each fennel and caraway seeds

½ teaspoon dried chilli flakes

420g (13½ ounces) lamb backstrap (eye of loin)

2 teaspoons olive oil

1 clove garlic, crushed

2 tablespoons olive oil, extra

1 tablespoon lemon juice

1 pitta pocket bread (75g)

400g (12½ ounces) canned chickpeas (garbanzo beans), rinsed, drained

150g (4½ ounces) baby spinach leaves

1 cup loosely packed mint leaves

4 red radishes (140g), sliced thinly

2 shallots (50g), sliced thinly

1 cup loosely packed mint leaves

1 Rub spices all over lamb; season. Heat oil in a medium frying pan; cook lamb about 3 minutes each side or until browned and cooked as desired. Cover; stand 5 minutes, then slice thinly on the diagonal.
2 Meanwhile, combine garlic, extra oil and juice in a small bowl; season.
3 Cook pitta bread on a heated oiled grill plate (or grill or barbecue) over high heat about 30 seconds each side or until toasted; break into pieces.
4 Place lamb in a large serving dish with the bread, dressing and remaining ingredients; toss gently to combine.

prep + cook time 30 minutes **serves** 4
nutritional count per serving 19.8g total fat (4.2g saturated fat); 1675kJ (400 cal); 22.5g carbohydrate; 30.5g protein; 5.5g fibre

note Orecchiette is a traditional pasta from southern Italy's Puglia region, where it is made from semolina, and is served with oil, sausage and leafy greens. It is named after its shape (from the Italian meaning 'little ears') as it resembles tiny ears. Because of its chewy texture it is good in salads, but its concave shape is also good for holding pasta sauces.

spicy pasta with lamb, anchovies and rosemary

450g (14½ ounces) mint and rosemary lamb sausages

2 teaspoons olive oil

375g (12 ounces) orecchiette pasta

⅓ cup (80ml) olive oil, extra

2 cloves garlic, crushed

4 drained anchovy fillets (12g), chopped coarsely

1 fresh long red chilli, sliced thinly

1 teaspoon coarsely chopped fresh rosemary

2 large roma (egg) tomatoes (180g), chopped finely

100g (3 ounces) rocket leaves (arugula)

⅔ cup (50g) shaved parmesan cheese

1 Squeeze sausage meat from casings; discard casings. Break meat into small pieces.
2 Heat half the oil in a large frying pan over high heat; cook lamb until browned all over and cooked through. Remove from pan; drain on absorbent paper. Cover to keep warm.
3 Meanwhile, cook pasta in a large saucepan of boiling water until tender. Drain, reserving ½ cup of the cooking liquid. Return pasta to pan; cover to keep warm.
4 Heat extra oil in same cleaned frying pan over medium heat; cook garlic, anchovies, chilli and rosemary until chilli is soft. Add tomato; cook until heated through.
5 Add tomato mixture to pasta with lamb, rocket, reserved cooking liquid and ½ cup of the cheese; toss well. Season to taste. Serve pasta topped with remaining cheese.

prep + cook time 20 minutes **serves** 4
nutritional count per serving 46.6g total fat (17.7g saturated fat); 3591kJ (858 cal); 76.4g carbohydrate; 31.5g protein; 4.5g fibre

tip You can use any Italian-style sausages in this recipe.

READY IN 20 MINUTES

spring grilled lamb and warm pea salad

600g (1¼ pounds) lamb fillets

⅓ cup (80ml) extra virgin olive oil

1 teaspoon celery salt

1 stalk celery (150g), trimmed, sliced thinly

½ medium red onion (85g), sliced thinly

3 medium tomatoes (450g), sliced thinly

⅓ cup coarsely chopped fresh flat-leaf parsley

1 tablespoon lemon juice

1 cup (150g) shelled fresh peas

200g (6½ ounces) sugar snap peas, trimmed

1 Combine the lamb and 1 tablespoon of the oil in a medium bowl; toss to coat. Sprinkle lamb with celery salt.
2 Cook lamb on a heated oiled grill plate (or grill or barbecue) about 3 minutes each side or until cooked as desired. Cover; stand 10 minutes, then slice thickly.
3 Meanwhile, combine celery, onion, tomato, parsley, juice and remaining oil in a large bowl; season to taste.
4 Add peas to a medium saucepan of boiling water; boil, uncovered, 2 minutes. Add sugar snap peas; boil, uncovered, about 1 minute or until bright green. Drain well.
5 Add hot peas and lamb to salad mixture; toss gently to combine. Accompany salad with crusty bread or char-grilled bread slices, if you like.

prep + cook time 25 minutes **serves** 4
nutritional count per serving 27.4g total fat (6g saturated fat); 1864kJ (445 cal); 9.1g carbohydrate; 37.9g protein; 6.6g fibre

tips Shelled peas are available from some greengrocers. If unavailable, you will need to shell about 500g (1 pound) peas in the pod, or use frozen peas.
We used a variety of heirloom tomatoes (such as oxheart or beefsteak) here; they are available from selected greengrocers. If you can't find them, any tomato will do – vine-ripened tomatoes will give a better flavour. For a more vibrant salad, use a variety of colours.

lamb and harissa yogurt wraps

600g (1¼ pounds) lamb backstrap (eye of loin)

2 tablespoons moroccan seasoning

2 tablespoons extra virgin olive oil

8 small bread wraps (250g)

1 cup (185g) tabbouleh

1 tablespoon lemon juice

1 cup (280g) greek-style yogurt

2 tablespoons harissa

1 small red onion (100g), sliced thinly

6 red radishes (200g), sliced thinly

2 large roma (egg) tomatoes (180g), sliced thinly

⅓ cup lightly packed fresh coriander leaves (cilantro)

1 Sprinkle lamb all over with the seasoning. Heat half the oil in a medium frying pan over medium heat; cook lamb about 3 minutes each side or until cooked as desired. Cover; stand 10 minutes, then slice thinly.
2 Place wraps in a dry medium frying pan; warm wraps over medium heat about 1 minute each side or until heated through.
3 Combine tabbouleh, juice and the remaining oil in a medium bowl; season to taste.
4 Combine yogurt and harissa in a small bowl.
5 Serve lamb with warm wraps, onion, radish, tabbouleh, tomato, harissa yogurt and coriander.

prep + cook time 25 minutes **serves** 4
nutritional count per serving 23.1g total fat (7.7g saturated fat); 2638kJ (630 cal); 53.4g carbohydrate; 50.6g protein; 7.4g fibre

tips Lamb fillets or minced (ground) lamb could be used in this recipe. All types of bread wraps are suitable for this recipe. We used mild harissa in this recipe. If using the traditional hot harissa in a tube, start with 2 teaspoons and increase the amount according to your heat tolerance.

spring grilled lamb and warm pea salad

lamb and harissa yogurt wraps

lamb 71

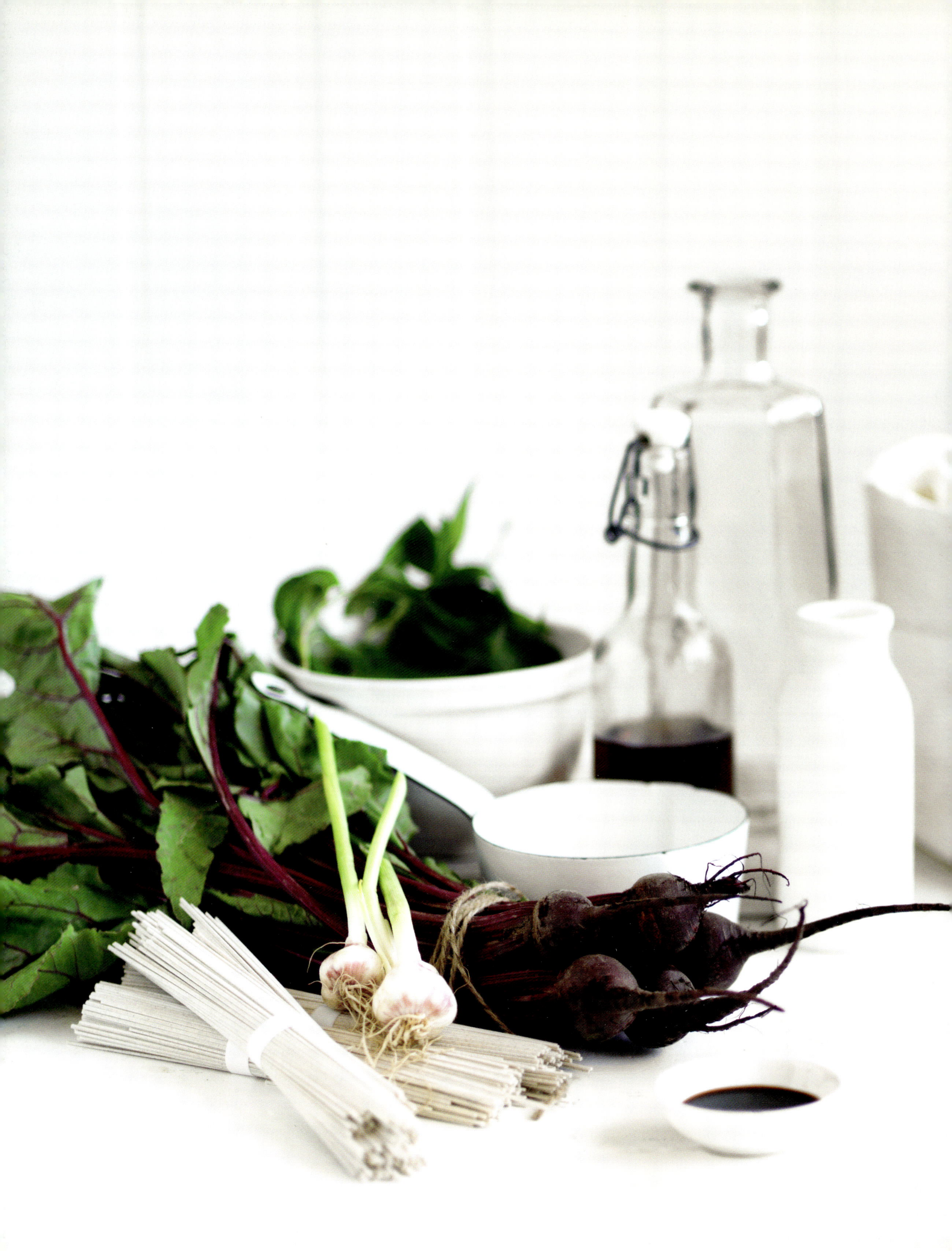

beef & veal

Beef and veal are excellent choices for dinner ideas – stir-fries, grills, pastas, burgers and salads are all on the menu.

steak and chips with a modern twist

1 small potato (120g)

1 small kumara (orange sweet potato) (250g)

2 small parsnips (240g), quartered lengthways

vegetable oil, for shallow-frying

2 tablespoons olive oil

4 x 200g (6½-ounce) porterhouse steaks

200g (6½ ounces) thinly sliced swiss brown mushrooms

300ml (½ pint) pouring cream

60g (2 ounces) baby spinach leaves

1 Using a mandoline or sharp knife, cut potato and kumara into 2mm (⅛-inch) thick slices.
2 Heat enough vegetable oil in a large frying pan to come 2cm (¾-inch) up the side of the pan; shallow-fry potato, kumara and parsnip, over medium heat, in batches, about 4 minutes or until golden and crisp. Drain on absorbent paper; season to taste.
3 Meanwhile, heat 1 tablespoon of the olive oil in a large frying pan over medium heat; cook beef about 5 minutes each side or until cooked as desired. Remove from pan; cover to keep warm.
4 Meanwhile, heat remaining olive oil in same pan; cook mushrooms over medium heat, stirring, about 4 minutes or until tender. Add cream, bring to the boil; simmer 3 minutes or until thickened and reduced slightly. Add spinach leaves; stir until just wilted.
5 Serve steaks topped with mushroom sauce and chips.

prep + cook time 30 minutes **serves** 4
nutritional count per serving 101.5g total fat (40.9g saturated fat); 5573kJ (1331 cal); 24.1g carbohydrate; 80.6g protein; 5.2g fibre

READY IN
30
MINUTES

READY IN 30 MINUTES

READY IN 20 MINUTES

blue-cheese-stuffed beef with brandied figs

prosciutto-wrapped cutlets with truss tomatoes

beef & veal

blue-cheese-stuffed beef with brandied figs

4 x 250g (8-ounce) beef sirloin steaks

200g (6½ ounces) firm blue cheese, sliced thinly

2 tablespoons olive oil

4 medium figs (240g), halved

¼ cup (110g) caster (superfine) sugar

170g (5½ ounces) asparagus, trimmed, sliced lengthways

½ cup (125ml) brandy

1 Preheat oven to 200°C/400°F.
2 Using a sharp knife, cut along the length of one side of each steak, three-quarters of the way through, to form a pocket. Fill pockets with cheese; secure with a toothpick.
3 Heat 1 tablespoon of the oil in a large frying pan; cook beef about 3 minutes each side or until browned. Place beef on an oiled oven tray; transfer to oven, bake about 15 minutes or until cooked as desired.
4 Meanwhile, sprinkle cut sides of figs with sugar.
5 Heat remaining oil in same frying pan; cook figs, cut-side down, with asparagus until figs begin to caramelise. Add brandy; cook until mixture reduces and thickens slightly, and becomes slightly syrupy.
6 Remove toothpicks from beef; serve beef with figs and asparagus; drizzle with brandy syrup.

prep + cook time 30 minutes **serves** 4
nutritional count per serving 51.5g total fat (23.6g saturated fat); 4584kJ (1095 cal); 39.7g carbohydrate; 110.5g protein; 2.6g fibre

serving suggestion Serve with sautéed potatoes (page 230).

prosciutto-wrapped cutlets with truss tomatoes

2 tablespoons dijon mustard

4 veal cutlets (1kg)

8 fresh sage leaves

4 slices prosciutto (60g)

500g (1 pound) truss cherry tomatoes

1½ tablespoons olive oil

¼ cup (60ml) balsamic vinegar

¾ cup (180ml) chicken stock

1 Preheat oven to 200°C/400°F.
2 Spread mustard on one side of each veal cutlet; top with sage leaves. Wrap a slice of prosciutto around each cutlet; secure with a toothpick.
3 Place tomatoes on a baking-paper-lined oven tray. Drizzle with 2 teaspoons of the oil; season. Roast about 12 minutes or until skins start to split.
4 Meanwhile, heat remaining oil in a large frying pan over medium heat; cook veal about 5 minutes each side or until browned and cooked as desired. Remove from pan, cover; stand 5 minutes.
5 Add vinegar to same pan; simmer 2 minutes or until syrupy. Add chicken stock to pan; simmer 3 minutes or until reduced by half. Serve veal with tomatoes; drizzle over sauce.

prep + cook time 20 minutes **serves** 4
nutritional count per serving 13.6g total fat (3.8g saturated fat); 1459kJ (348 cal); 3.7g carbohydrate; 51g protein; 2g fibre

serving suggestion Potato purée (see page 216).

beef and mixed sprout salad

4cm (1½-inch) piece fresh ginger (20g), grated finely

2 cloves garlic, crushed

1 tablespoon soy sauce

2 tablespoons olive oil

600g (1¼ pounds) beef rump steak

1 medium carrot (120g), grated coarsely

½ cup (20g) alfalfa sprouts

½ cup (25g) snow pea sprouts

250g (8 ounces) baby spinach leaves

soy lime dressing

2 tablespoons lime juice

1 tablespoon olive oil

1 tablespoon soy sauce

1 Combine ginger, garlic, soy sauce and half the oil in a medium bowl. Add beef; turn to coat in marinade.
2 Cook beef on a heated oiled grill plate (or grill or barbecue) about 3 minutes each side or until cooked as desired. Cover; refrigerate 10 minutes.
3 Meanwhile, make soy lime dressing.
4 Cut cooled beef into thin strips. Serve beef strips with carrot, sprouts and spinach; drizzle with dressing. Accompany with lime cheeks, if you like.
soy lime dressing Place ingredients in a screw-top jar; shake well to combine.

prep + cook time 30 minutes **serves** 4
nutritional count per serving 28g total fat (7.5g saturated fat); 2012kJ (481 cal); 2.8g carbohydrate; 53g protein; 2.8g fibre

READY IN 30 MINUTES

READY IN
20 MINUTES

tip If you like, buy fried shallot (homm jiew) instead of making your own. It is regularly used on Asian tables as a condiment or sprinkled over cooked dishes. It can be purchased in cellophane bags at Asian grocery stores; once opened, fried shallot will keep for months if tightly sealed.

T-bone steaks with crispy shallots and horseradish mascarpone

¼ cup (60ml) olive oil

4 shallots (100g), sliced thinly

4 beef T-bone steaks (striploin) (1.2kg)

horseradish mascarpone
60g (2 ounces) spreadable cream cheese
1 tablespoon horseradish cream
¼ teaspoon cracked black pepper
¼ cup (60g) mascarpone cheese

1 Heat the oil in a deep large frying pan over high heat; cook shallots about 2 minutes or until browned and crisp. Drain on absorbent paper. Drain oil from pan.
2 Heat same pan; cook beef about 3 minutes or until browned both sides and cooked as desired. Cover; stand 5 minutes.
3 Meanwhile, make horseradish mascarpone.
4 Serve beef with horseradish mascarpone; sprinkle with crispy shallots.
horseradish mascarpone Beat cream cheese, horseradish and pepper in a small bowl until combined. Stir in mascarpone.

prep + cook time 20 minutes **serves** 4
nutritional count per serving 51.8g total fat (20.9g saturated fat); 2723kJ (650 cal); 2.5g carbohydrate; 44.7g protein; 0.5g fibre

serving suggestion Serve with garlicky beans with pine nuts (page 225).

tip To toast nuts, place nuts in a single layer in a dry frying pan; stir over a low heat until fragrant and just changed in colour. Remove from pan immediately.

lemon and thyme veal cutlets with beetroot salad

4 x 200g (6½-ounce) veal cutlets

2 cloves garlic, crushed

1 tablespoon fresh thyme leaves

1 tablespoon lemon juice

1 tablespoon olive oil

170g (5½ ounces) asparagus, trimmed, halved lengthways

450g (14½ ounces) canned baby beetroot (beets), drained, halved

250g (8 ounces) rocket leaves (arugula)

½ cup (50g) toasted walnuts

120g (4 ounces) goat's cheese, crumbled

lemon dressing

1 medium lemon (140g)

1 tablespoon olive oil

1 Combine veal, garlic, thyme, juice and oil in a large bowl; stand 10 minutes.
2 Cook veal on a heated oiled grill plate (or grill or barbecue) about 3 minutes each side or until browned and cooked as desired. Cover; stand 5 minutes.
3 Meanwhile, cook asparagus on a grill plate (or grill or barbecue) about 2 minutes or until tender.
4 Make lemon dressing.
5 Place beetroot and asparagus in a large bowl with rocket and dressing; toss gently to combine. Top with walnuts and cheese.
6 Serve veal with beetroot salad, and lemon wedges, if you like.
lemon dressing Using a zester or small sharp knife, cut lemon rind into long thin strips. Juice lemon (you need 2 tablespoons juice). Combine ingredients in a screw-top jar; shake well.

prep + cook time 30 minutes **serves** 4
nutritional count per serving 27.7g total fat (7.8g saturated fat); 2073kJ (495 cal); 11.5g carbohydrate; 47.2g protein; 6.9g fibre

READY IN 30 MINUTES

READY IN 25 MINUTES

tips For a milder version, reduce the sambal oelek to 2 teaspoons. Chinese sausage is called lup chung or lap chong and is available from Asian butcher shops.

spicy beef kway teow

450g (14½ ounces) thick fresh rice noodles

400g (12½ ounces) beef fillet, sliced thinly

3 cloves garlic, crushed

3cm (1¼-inch) piece fresh ginger (15g), grated finely

1 tablespoon sambal oelek

2 tablespoons peanut oil

2 chinese sausages (60g), sliced thinly on the diagonal

2 tablespoons salt-reduced soy sauce

2 tablespoons kecap manis

2 eggs, beaten lightly

1½ cups (120g) bean sprouts

3 green onions (scallions), sliced thinly on the diagonal

1 fresh long red chilli, sliced thinly

1 Prepare noodles following instructions on the packet.
2 Combine beef, garlic, ginger and sambal oelek in a medium bowl.
3 Heat half the oil in a wok over high heat; stir-fry beef, in batches, until browned and cooked as desired. Remove from wok.
4 Heat remaining oil in wok; stir-fry sausages until crisp. Return beef to wok with noodles and sauces; stir-fry about 2 minutes or until heated through. Add egg; stir-fry 30 seconds. Add two-thirds of the sprouts and the onion; stir-fry until the egg is just cooked.
5 Serve stir-fry sprinkled with the remaining sprouts, remaining onion and chilli.

prep + cook time 25 minutes **serves** 4
nutritional count per serving 33g total fat (10.5g saturated fat); 2248kJ (585 cal); 24.4g carbohydrate; 46.5g protein; 2.2g fibre

tip Chinese cooking wine is also known as shoa xing or shao hsing. It is readily available from Asian supermarkets. If you can't find it, replace it with mirin or dry sherry.

sichuan beef stir-fry

3 teaspoons sichuan peppercorns

500g (1 pound) sliced beef fillet steak

2 tablespoons peanut oil

100g (3 ounces) baby corn, halved lengthways

30g (1 ounces) each oyster and shiitake mushrooms, sliced thinly

100g (3 ounces) broccolini, cut into 5cm (2-inch) lengths

100g (3 ounces) gai lan, cut into 5cm (2-inch) lengths

2 tablespoons soy sauce

1½ tablespoons chinese cooking wine

1 Stir-fry pepper in a dry wok over high heat about 2 minutes or until fragrant. Remove from wok; crush with grinder or mortar and pestle. Combine pepper and beef in a medium bowl with half the oil; turn to coat beef in mixture.
2 Stir-fry beef, in batches, over high heat, about 2 minutes or until just browned. Remove from wok; cover to keep warm.
3 Heat remaining oil in wok; stir-fry corn and mushrooms 2 minutes or until almost tender. Add broccolini and gai lan; stir-fry 1 minute or until gai lan just begins to wilt. Return beef to wok with sauce and wine, tossing to combine.

prep + cook time 25 minutes **serves** 4
nutritional count per serving 28.9g total fat; (9.4g saturated fat); 2000kJ (478 cal); 5.3g carbohydrate; 48.2g protein; 2.2g fibre

serving suggestion Steamed jasmine rice.

READY IN 25 MINUTES

READY IN
30
MINUTES

creamy beef and mushroom rigatoni

500g (1 pound) rigatoni pasta

600g (1¼ pounds) beef fillet steak, sliced thinly

¼ cup (35g) plain (all-purpose) flour

2 tablespoons olive oil

20g (¾ ounce) butter

4 shallots (100g), sliced thinly

2 cloves garlic, crushed

375g (12 ounces) button mushrooms, quartered

⅓ cup (80ml) brandy

2 cups (500ml) beef stock

1¼ cups (300g) sour cream

¼ cup coarsely chopped fresh flat-leaf parsley

¼ cup (20g) finely grated parmesan cheese

2 tablespoons torn fresh flat-leaf parsley leaves, extra

1 Cook pasta in a large saucepan of boiling water until tender; drain.
2 Meanwhile, coat beef in flour; shake off excess flour. Heat oil in a large saucepan over high heat; cook beef, in batches, until browned. Remove from pan, cover to keep warm.
3 Melt butter in the same pan; cook shallot, garlic and mushrooms, stirring occasionally, until softened. Add brandy; cook, stirring, 30 seconds.
4 Add stock to pan; bring to the boil. Reduce heat; simmer, covered, 5 minutes. Add beef and sour cream to pan; stir until smooth. Remove from heat; season to taste. Add pasta and parsley; stir until combined.
5 Serve pasta sprinkled with cheese and extra parsley.

prep + cook time 30 minutes **serves** 6
nutritional count per serving 48.9g total fat (23.6g saturated fat); 3945kJ (943 cal); 69.1g carbohydrate; 51.4g protein; 4.1g fibre

tip To save time, ask the butcher to slice the beef.

beef & veal

beef quesadillas

vietnamese beef salad

beef quesadillas

1 medium avocado (250g), chopped coarsely

1 tablespoon lemon juice

1 tablespoon vegetable oil

500g (1 pound) minced (ground) beef

2 teaspoons ground cumin

400g (12½ ounces) canned kidney beans, drained, rinsed

3 medium roma (egg) tomatoes (225g), chopped finely

3 green onions (scallions), sliced thinly

8 x 19cm (7¾-inch) flour tortillas

1 cup (120g) grated cheddar cheese

¼ cup (60g) sour cream

1 medium lemon (140g), cut into wedges

1 Using a fork, mash the avocado and juice together in a small bowl. Season to taste.
2 Heat oil in a large frying pan; cook the beef, stirring, until browned. Add cumin; cook, stirring, 1 minute or until fragrant. Stir in the beans, tomato and onion. Remove pan from heat.
3 Divide beef mixture among four tortillas; sprinkle with cheese. Top with remaining tortillas. Cook one at a time in a preheated sandwich press, for about 2 minutes or until cheese is melted and tortillas are browned lightly.
4 Cut quesadillas into quarters; serve with avocado mixture, sour cream and lemon wedges.

prep + cook time 25 minutes **serves** 4
nutritional count per serving 50.4g total fat (21.4g saturated fat); 3329kJ (795 cal); 32.8g carbohydrate; 49.2g protein; 8.3g fibre

tip If you don't have a sandwich press, cook these in a large frying pan or grill pan. Cook one at a time, over medium-low heat, about 2 minutes each side. Use two spatulas to carefully flip quesadillas.
serving suggestion Leafy green salad.

vietnamese beef salad

1 tablespoon peanut oil

800g (1½ pounds) trimmed beef fillet steak

½ cup (125ml) vietnamese dressing

400g (12½ ounces) mixed cherry tomatoes, halved

280g (9 ounces) packaged salad leaf mix

1 cup firmly packed fresh vietnamese mint leaves

1 Heat oil in a medium frying pan; cook the beef for about 3 minutes on each side or until cooked as desired. Transfer to a large plate; drizzle with 2 tablespoons of the dressing. Cover; stand 5 minutes, then slice thinly.
2 Combine tomato, salad leaves, mint and remaining dressing in a large bowl; season. Serve salad topped with beef.

prep + cook time 20 minutes **serves** 6
nutritional count per serving 24g total fat (8.8g saturated fat); 1849kJ (442 cal); 6.1g carbohydrate; 49.8g protein; 1.2g fibre

tip You can use regular mint instead of the vietnamese mint if it is hard to find.

tip If you prefer not to use the microwave rice, you can boil, steam or microwave ¾ cup (150g) basmati rice for this recipe.

upside-down beef

¼ cup (60ml) peanut oil

350g (11 ounces) beef strips

1 teaspoon minced garlic

1 teaspoon minced ginger

1 teaspoon cornflour (cornstarch)

¼ cup (60ml) water

100g (3 ounces) sliced swiss brown mushrooms

4 green onions (scallions), cut into 5cm (2-inch) lengths

2 tablespoons oyster sauce

2 tablespoons soy sauce

1 teaspoon white (granulated) sugar

500g (1 pound) packet basmati 90-second microwave rice

2 eggs

1 Heat 1 tablespoon of the oil in a wok over high heat; stir-fry beef, garlic and ginger until beef is browned all over. Remove from wok; cover to keep warm.
2 Combine cornflour and the water in a small jug.
3 Heat half the remaining oil in wok; stir-fry mushrooms until tender. Return beef to wok with onion, combined sauces, sugar and cornflour mixture; stir-fry until beef is tender and sauce is slightly thickened. Remove from heat; cover to keep warm.
4 Cook rice in microwave oven following packet instructions.
5 Heat the remaining oil in a large frying pan over medium heat; cook eggs until cooked as desired.
6 Place fried eggs, yolk-side down, into two deep 2-cup (500ml) bowls; divide stir-fry and rice evenly between bowls. Press down firmly, but not so hard that the yolk breaks. Cover each bowl with a serving plate, invert onto the plate. Serve with sweet chilli sauce, if you like.

prep + cook time 20 minutes **serves** 2
nutritional count per serving 36.8g total fat (8g saturated fat); 3652kJ (872 cal); 76.5g carbohydrate; 57.3g protein; 2.6g fibre

serving suggestion Steamed gai lan in oyster sauce (page 226).

READY IN
20
MINUTES

READY IN
30
MINUTES

note Fajita is a traditional Mexican dish where grilled meats and vegetables are rolled up in a tortilla and eaten with your hands. Chicken or pork may be used instead of the beef.

beef fajitas

1 large tomato (220g), chopped finely
1 fresh long green chilli, chopped finely
2 green onions (scallions), chopped finely
1 tablespoon lime juice
½ cup coarsely chopped fresh coriander (cilantro)
2 tablespoons olive oil
1 large brown onion (200g), sliced thickly
2 small red capsicums (bell pepper) (300g), sliced thinly
400g (12½ ounces) rump steak, sliced thinly
40g (1½-ounce) packet fajita spice mix
150g (4½ ounces) snow peas, sliced thinly
3 cloves garlic, crushed
8 tortillas

1 To make salsa, place tomato, chilli, green onion, juice and coriander in a medium bowl; season. Toss gently to combine.
2 Heat half the oil in a large frying pan over high heat; cook brown onion and capsicum, stirring, until browned lightly and softened. Remove from pan.
3 Heat remaining oil in same pan; cook beef, in two batches, until browned. Return onion mixture to pan with beef, spice mix, peas and garlic; cook, stirring, until fragrant and peas are bright green.
4 Serve beef mixture with tortillas and salsa; accompany with lime wedges, if you like.

prep + cook time 30 minutes **makes** 8
nutritional count per serving 11.6g total fat (2.9g saturated fat); 1071kJ (256 cal); 15.1g carbohydrate; 20.8g protein; 4.1g fibre

warm roast beef and vegetable salad

650g (1¼ pounds) beef eye fillet

2 tablespoons olive oil

2 teaspoons wholegrain mustard

4 small beetroot (beets) (400g)

2 small kumara (orange sweet potato) (500g), cut into wedges

400g (12½ ounces) baby carrots, trimmed

1 medium red onion (170g), cut into wedges

250g (8 ounces) baby red capsicums (bell peppers), halved, seeded

170g (5½ ounces) asparagus, trimmed

60g (2 ounces) baby spinach leaves

mustard horseradish dressing

2 teaspoons horseradish cream

1 small clove garlic, crushed

2 teaspoons wholegrain mustard

2 teaspoons red wine vinegar

¼ cup (60ml) olive oil

2 tablespoons light thickened (heavy) cream

1 Preheat oven to 240°C/475°F.
2 Rub beef all over with half the oil. Cook beef in a heated flameproof baking dish over high heat on the stove top until browned all over. Spread mustard all over beef; season. Transfer to oven; roast, uncovered, about 15 minutes or until beef is cooked as desired. Remove beef from dish; cover to keep warm.
3 Meanwhile, trim beetroot; cut in half (or quarters if large), then wrap in foil; enclose to form a parcel. Roast beetroot in baking dish with beef for the last 10 minutes of beef cooking time.
4 Place kumara, carrots, onion and capsicum on baking-paper-lined large oven tray; transfer beetroot, still in foil, to tray with vegetables. Brush vegetables with remaining oil; season. Roast vegetables about 15 minutes or until tender and beginning to brown. Remove vegetables from tray as they are cooked.
5 Add asparagus to oven tray for last 5 minutes of cooking time or until just tender.
6 Make mustard horseradish dressing. Peel beetroot.
7 Place spinach on a serving platter; top with warm roast vegetables, drizzle with a little dressing. Slice beef thickly; arrange on top of vegetables; drizzle with dressing.
mustard horseradish dressing Whisk horseradish cream, garlic, mustard and vinegar in a medium bowl until combined. Gradually whisk in oil then cream. Season to taste.

prep + cook time 35 minutes **serves** 4
nutritional count per serving 20.6g total fat (14.9g saturated fat); 3624kJ (866 cal); 32.6g carbohydrate; 65.7g protein; 11.4g fibre

tips Dressing can be made a day ahead. If your oven or oven tray is small, place the capsicum in the baking dish with the beef. The vegetables should be spread out in a single layer so they cook quickly.

READY IN
35
MINUTES

READY IN
30 MINUTES

thai spicy beef and noodle stir-fry

200g (6½ ounces) dry rice noodles

1 tablespoon peanut oil

500g (1 pound) rump steak, sliced thinly

3 cloves garlic, crushed

2 fresh small red thai (serrano) chillies, chopped finely

2 tablespoons fish sauce

2 tablespoons dark soy sauce

1 tablespoon light brown sugar

4 kaffir lime leaves, shredded

3 medium tomatoes (450g), chopped finely

¼ cup fresh coriander (cilantro) leaves

1 Cook noodles according to directions on packet; drain.
2 Heat half the oil in a wok over high heat; stir-fry beef, in batches, until browned. Remove from wok; cover to keep warm.
3 Heat remaining oil in wok; stir-fry garlic and chilli until fragrant. Add sauces, sugar and lime leaves; stir-fry until combined.
4 Return beef to wok with noodles and tomato; stir-fry until tomato starts to soften and is heated through. Serve sprinkled with coriander.

prep + cook time 30 minutes **serves** 4
nutritional count per serving 16.6g total fat (5.3g saturated fat); 1692kJ (404 cal); 16.7g carbohydrate; 45.3g protein; 2.8g fibre

READY IN 20 MINUTES

sausage and crunchy slaw burgers

8 thick beef sausages (1kg)

¼ cup (70g) tomato sauce (ketchup)

¼ cup (70g) barbecue sauce

2 tablespoons sweet chilli sauce

¼ small red cabbage (300g), shredded finely

¼ small green cabbage (300g), shredded finely

2 green onions (scallions), sliced thinly

1 small carrot (70g), grated coarsely

¾ cup (225g) mayonnaise

2 tablespoons wholegrain mustard

1 tablespoon lemon juice

8 bread rolls (50g)

1 Split sausages lengthways without cutting all the way through; open out flat. Place sausages, cut-side down, on grill tray or wire rack over an oven tray.
2 Preheat grill (broiler).
3 Combine sauces in a small bowl; brush half the sauce mixture over sausages. Cook sausages under grill until well browned. Turn, brush with remaining sauce mixture; grill until browned and cooked through. Transfer to a plate; cover to keep warm.
4 Meanwhile, combine cabbages, onion and carrot in a large bowl; season to taste.
5 Combine mayonnaise, mustard and juice in a small bowl.
6 Split rolls, without cutting all the way through; toast under hot grill until browned lightly both sides.
7 Divide sausages, slaw and mayonnaise between rolls.

prep + cook time 20 minutes **makes** 8
nutritional count per serving 57.9g total fat (15.5g saturated fat); 3236kJ (773 cal); 39.1g carbohydrate; 22.1g protein; 7.5g fibre

tip Shred the cabbage with a mandoline or V-slicer.

tips Add or omit the chilli to taste. The heat from the soup cooks the beef. Thai basil is also known as horapa; it has smallish leaves and a sweet licorice/aniseed taste. It is available from Asian greengrocers and some supermarkets.

quick beef pho

2 litres (8 cups) salt-reduced beef stock

2 cups (500ml) water

4cm (1½-inch) piece fresh ginger (20g), sliced thinly

2 cloves garlic, sliced thinly

2 star anise

2 cinnamon sticks

400g (12½ ounces) rice stick noodles

400g (12½ ounces) beef eye fillet, sliced very thinly

⅓ cup (80ml) fish sauce

2 tablespoons brown sugar

4 green onions (scallions), sliced thinly

1 cup (80g) bean sprouts

2 fresh small red thai (serrano) chillies, sliced thinly

⅓ cup each lightly packed fresh thai basil and mint sprigs

1 medium lemon (140g), cut into wedges

1 Place stock, the water, ginger, garlic, star anise and cinnamon in a large saucepan; bring to the boil. Reduce heat; simmer, covered, 15 minutes. Remove ginger and spices from pan with a slotted spoon.
2 Meanwhile, add noodles to a large saucepan of boiling water. Remove from heat; stand 5 minutes. Drain.
3 Divide noodles among serving bowls, top with beef.
4 Stir fish sauce, sugar and onion into the stock mixture; bring to a simmer. Season to taste.
5 Ladle hot soup mixture over beef in bowls; top with sprouts, chilli and herbs. Serve with lemon wedges.

prep + cook time 25 minutes **serves** 4
nutritional count per serving 18.1g total fat (6.8g saturated fat); 2038kJ (487 cal); 33.7g carbohydrate; 45.4g protein; 3.3g fibre

READY IN
25
MINUTES

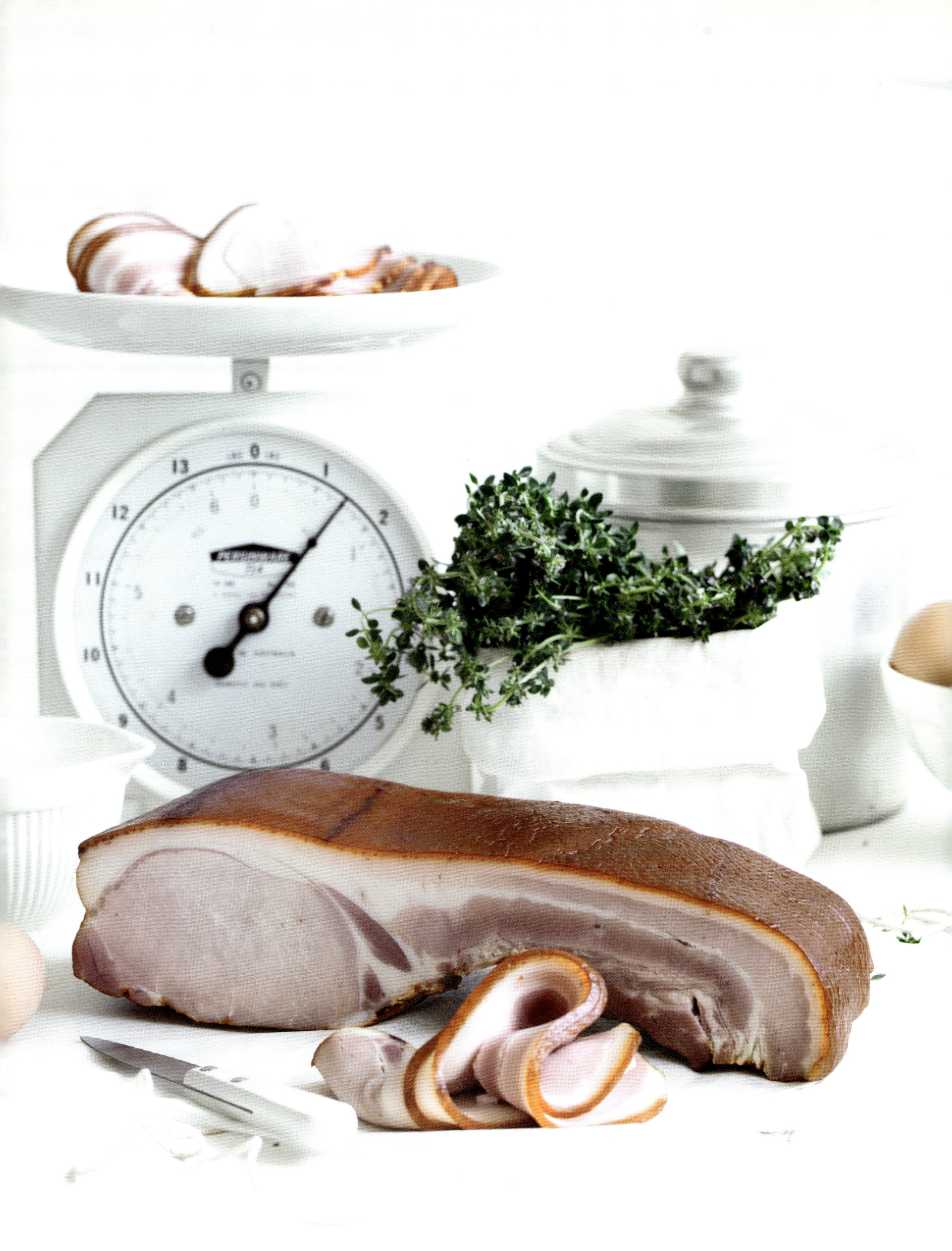

pork

Known as the 'other white meat', pork is a popular meat that blends well with many spices, giving it an added depth of flavour.

tip Uncooked meatballs can be frozen for up to three months; place in an airtight container, separating the layers with baking paper to prevent them sticking together.

pork and rosemary meatballs with pasta

375g (12 ounces) angel hair pasta

500g (1 pound) minced (ground) pork

1 large brown onion (200g), chopped finely

2 cloves garlic, crushed

¼ cup (15g) stale breadcrumbs

1 egg, beaten lightly

1½ tablespoons coarsely chopped fresh rosemary

1 tablespoon olive oil

1 tablespoon tomato paste

½ cup (125ml) dry red wine

700g (1½ pounds) bottled tomato pasta sauce

1 cup (250ml) water

⅓ cup (25g) finely grated parmesan cheese

1 Cook pasta in a large saucepan of boiling water until tender; drain. Cover to keep warm.

2 Combine pork, half the onion, half the garlic, the breadcrumbs, egg and rosemary in a large bowl. Using damp hands, roll heaped tablespoons of mixture into balls.

3 Heat the oil in a large saucepan; cook the remaining onion and garlic, stirring, until onion softens. Stir in paste; cook, stirring, 2 minutes. Add the wine, pasta sauce and the water; bring to the boil.

4 Carefully drop the meatballs into the sauce; simmer for about 10 minutes or until meatballs are cooked through.

5 Serve pasta topped with meatballs, sprinkle with cheese.

prep + cook time 30 minutes **serves** 4
nutritional count per serving 21.6g total fat (7.2g saturated fat); 3156kJ (754 cal); 85.5g carbohydrate; 46.4g protein; 1.3g fibre

READY IN
30 MINUTES

READY IN
30
MINUTES

READY IN
20
MINUTES

pork cutlets with baked parsnips and apples

sweet and sticky ginger pork cutlets

pork cutlets with baked parsnips and apples

4 small parsnips (480g), peeled, halved lengthways

3 small red apples (390g), unpeeled, quartered

4 cloves garlic, unpeeled

¼ cup loosely packed sage leaves

2 tablespoons pure maple syrup

¼ cup (60ml) olive oil

250g (8 ounces) apple sauce

4 x 200g (6½-ounce) pork cutlets

1 Preheat oven to 200°C/400°F.
2 Combine parsnip, apple, garlic, sage, syrup and 2 tablespoons of the oil in a large baking dish. Bake about 20 minutes or until vegetables are tender.
3 Meanwhile, heat sauce in a small saucepan over low heat until just warmed. Cover to keep warm.
4 Heat remaining oil on a grill plate (or grill or barbecue); cook pork for about 4 minutes on each side or until browned and cooked as desired.
5 Serve pork with warm apple sauce and baked vegetables.

prep + cook time 30 minutes **serves** 4
nutritional count per serving 16.3g total fat (3g saturated fat); 1910kJ (456 cal); 43.7g carbohydrate; 30.9g protein; 7.9g fibre

tip You can use apple sauce or apple puree in this recipe.
serving suggestion Brussels sprouts with cream and almonds (page 221).

sweet and sticky ginger pork cutlets

2 tablespoons olive oil

4 x 235g (7½-ounce) pork cutlets

2 medium apples (300g), unpeeled

1 tablespoon soy sauce

4cm (1½-inch) piece fresh ginger (20g), grated finely

2 tablespoons brown sugar

2 teaspoons finely grated orange rind

1 cup (250ml) orange juice

1 Heat half the oil in a large frying pan over medium heat; cook pork about 4 minutes each side or until browned and cooked as desired. Remove from pan; cover to keep warm.
2 Slice apples into 1cm (½-inch) thick rounds. Heat remaining oil in same pan; cook apples, turning occasionally, until just tender but still hold their shape. Remove from pan.
3 Add soy sauce, ginger, sugar, rind and juice to pan; bring to the boil. Return pork and apples to pan, reduce heat; simmer for 5 minutes, turning occasionally, until sauce has thickened.

prep + cook time 20 minutes **serves** 4
nutritional count per serving 14.1g total fat (3g saturated fat); 1773kJ (424 cal); 20.4g carbohydrate; 52.9g protein; 2.1g fibre

tip You can use either red or green apples in this recipe.
serving suggestion Steamed asian greens with char siu sauce (page 227).

note Taleggio cheese is a washed rind Italian cheese that has a strong aroma, but a comparatively mild taste. You can buy taleggio cheese from delicatessens or Italian grocers. If unavailable use fresh mozzarella or fontina.

taleggio, prosciutto and rocket pizzas

1 large red onion (300g), cut into thin wedges

1½ tablespoons balsamic vinegar

2 x 150g (4½-ounce) pizza bases

½ cup (130g) bottled tomato and basil pasta sauce

½ cup (50g) grated mozzarella cheese

½ cup (100g) drained roasted capsicum (bell pepper) strips

6 slices prosciutto (90g), torn roughly

150g (4½ ounces) taleggio cheese, torn

50g (1½ ounces) baby rocket leaves (arugula)

1 Preheat oven to 240°C/475°F.
2 Place the onion on a baking-paper-lined oven tray; drizzle with vinegar. Bake for about 15 minutes or until onion is tender.
3 Meanwhile, place pizza bases on two lightly greased oven trays; top with pasta sauce, mozzarella, capsicum, prosciutto and taleggio. Bake about 12 minutes or until cheese has melted and bases are crisp.
4 Combine rocket and baked onion in a medium bowl.
5 Cut pizzas into wedges; top with rocket mixture.

prep + cook time 25 minutes **serves** 4
nutritional count per serving 17g total fat (8.8g saturated fat); 1850kJ (442 cal); 42.2g carbohydrate; 27g protein; 5.1g fibre

READY IN 25 MINUTES

READY IN
30
MINUTES

READY IN
30
MINUTES

pork, orange and coriander salad

pea, ham and mint soup

pork, orange and coriander salad

440g (14 ounces) pork fillet

2 tablespoons char siu sauce

2 medium oranges (480g)

1 fresh long green chilli, sliced thinly

100g (3 ounces) snow pea sprouts

100g (3 ounces) baby salad leaves

½ cup loosely packed fresh coriander leaves (cilantro)

⅓ cup (80ml) orange juice

2 tablespoons olive oil

1 Cut pork in half lengthways. Combine pork and sauce in a medium bowl; turn to coat in mixture.
2 Cook pork on a heated oiled grill plate (or grill or barbecue) for about 8 minutes each side or until cooked as desired. Remove from heat; cover to keep warm.
3 Meanwhile, segment oranges into a large bowl; add chilli, sprouts, salad leaves, coriander and combined juice and oil. Toss gently to combine.
4 Thinly slice the pork. Divide salad among serving bowls; top with pork.

prep + cook time 30 minutes **serves** 4
nutritional count per serving 10.6g total fat (1.9g saturated fat); 1152kJ (275 cal); 16.3g carbohydrate; 26.7g protein; 3.7g fibre

tip Baby salad leaves are also sold as salad mix or gourmet salad mix; it is a mixture of assorted young lettuce and other green leaves. You can use your favourite salad greens.

pea, ham and mint soup

1 tablespoon olive oil

250g (8 ounces) rindless bacon slices, chopped coarsely

1 medium leek (350g), trimmed, sliced thinly

1 stalk celery (150g), trimmed, sliced thinly

2 cloves garlic, crushed

880g (1¾ pounds) canned peas, drained

1 litre (4 cups) chicken stock

2 cups (500ml) water

1 cup firmly packed fresh mint leaves

1 Heat the oil in a large saucepan; cook bacon, leek, celery and garlic, stirring, until onion softens and bacon is golden.
2 Add peas to pan with remaining ingredients; bring to the boil. Reduce heat; simmer 20 minutes. Cool 10 minutes.
3 Blend or process soup, in batches, until almost smooth. Serve with a sprig of mint and a drizzle of oil, if you like.

prep + cook time 30 minutes **serves** 4
nutritional count per serving 24.3g total fat (7.8g saturated fat); 1625kJ (388 cal); 17.3g carbohydrate; 20.2g protein; 13.2g fibre

tip Wash the leek thoroughly under cold running water to remove any dirt between the layers.

READY IN
30 MINUTES

ricotta and sausage pasta

450g (14½ ounces) italian-style pork sausages

2 tablespoons olive oil

2 cloves garlic, chopped finely

½ teaspoon dried chilli flakes

½ teaspoon fennel seeds, crushed

800g (1½ pounds) canned diced tomatoes

375g (12 ounces) penne pasta

1½ tablespoons pine nuts

⅔ cup (50g) stale breadcrumbs

½ cup fresh basil leaves

⅔ cup (160g) ricotta cheese

1 Squeeze sausage meat from casings; discard casings.
2 Heat half the oil in a large saucepan over medium heat; cook sausage meat, garlic, chilli flakes and fennel seeds, stirring, about 5 minutes or until browned. Add tomatoes; bring to the boil. Reduce heat; simmer, uncovered, about 10 minutes or until thickened. Season to taste.
3 Meanwhile, cook pasta in a large saucepan of boiling water until just tender; drain.
4 Heat remaining oil in a small frying pan; cook pine nuts, stirring, until lightly golden. Add breadcrumbs; cook, stirring, until golden and crisp. Remove from heat.
5 Add pasta and basil to sauce; stir to combine. Divide pasta among serving bowls; top with cheese and breadcrumb mixture. Top with extra basil leaves, if you like.

prep + cook time 30 minutes **serves** 4
nutritional count per serving 38.2g total fat (12.3g saturated fat); 3485kJ (832cal); 86.5g carbohydrate; 31.9g protein; 6.8g fibre

pork steaks with sautéed lentils

2 tablespoons olive oil

1 medium red onion (170g), chopped finely

2 cloves garlic, crushed

6 slices pancetta (90g), chopped finely

1 tablespoon finely chopped fresh rosemary

3 sprigs fresh thyme

800g (1½ pounds) canned brown lentils, rinsed, drained

½ cup (125ml) water

1 tablespoon lemon juice

4 x 150g (4½-ounce) uncrumbed pork schnitzels

1 medium lemon (140g), cut into cheeks

1 Heat half the oil in a large frying pan over high heat; cook the onion, garlic and pancetta, stirring, until onion softens. Add herbs; cook, stirring, about 1 minute or until fragrant. Add the lentils and the water; reduce heat, simmer, uncovered, about 2 minutes or until the water evaporates. Stir in the juice.

2 Meanwhile, cut the pork in half crossways. Heat remaining oil in a large frying pan over medium heat; cook pork, in batches, until browned both sides and cooked as desired. Cover, stand 2 minutes.

3 Serve pork with lentils and lemon cheeks; accompany with steamed green beans, if you like.

prep + cook time 30 minutes **serves** 4
nutritional count per serving 5.3g total fat (3.6g saturated fat); 1915kJ (457 cal); 21.6g carbohydrate; 53.5g protein; 8.8g fibre

READY IN
30
MINUTES

puttanesca potato bake

bacon, leek and potato frittata

puttanesca potato bake

1.2kg (2½ pounds) baby new potatoes (chats), halved

cooking-oil spray

4 slices pancetta (60g)

2 cloves garlic, crushed

8 drained anchovy fillets (45g), chopped finely

400g (12½ ounces) canned crushed tomatoes

½ cup (75g) drained semi-dried tomatoes in oil

½ cup (75g) pitted black olives

⅓ cup coarsely chopped fresh flat-leaf parsley

1 cup (120g) grated cheddar cheese

2 tablespoons fresh flat-leaf parsley leaves, extra

1 Preheat grill (broiler). Grease a 3-litre (12-cup) ovenproof dish.
2 Boil, steam or microwave potatoes until tender.
3 Meanwhile, lightly spray a large frying pan with oil; heat over high heat. Cook pancetta, turning occasionally, until crisp. When cool enough to handle, coarsely chop pancetta.
4 Add garlic, anchovies and crushed tomatoes to same pan; bring to the boil. Remove pan from heat, add potatoes, semi-dried tomatoes, olives and parsley; stir to combine. Pour into dish; sprinkle with cheese.
5 Place under a hot grill for about 5 minutes or until golden. Serve sprinkled with pancetta and extra parsley.

prep + cook time 30 minutes **serves** 6
nutritional count per serving 12.6g total fat (5.9g saturated fat); 1365kJ (326 cal); 31.6g carbohydrate; 16.9g protein; 7.1g fibre

serving suggestion Leafy green salad.

bacon, leek and potato frittata

1 tablespoon olive oil

2 medium leeks (700g), trimmed, sliced thinly

3 rindless bacon slices (195g), chopped finely

cooking-oil spray

800g (1½ pounds) canned baby potatoes, drained, halved

1 tablespoon fresh thyme leaves

½ cup (40g) finely grated parmesan cheese

8 eggs, beaten lightly

⅓ cup (80ml) pouring cream

1 Preheat oven to 180°C/350°F.
2 Heat the oil in a deep 25cm (10-inch) ovenproof frying pan on stove top over high heat; cook leek and bacon, stirring, until leek is soft. Remove from pan.
3 Spray same pan with cooking oil. Place potatoes in pan; top with leek and bacon mixture. Sprinkle with thyme and cheese.
4 Combine eggs and cream in a large jug; season. Pour egg mixture over potatoes; cook, covered, over low heat about 10 minutes or until edges begin to set. Transfer pan to oven; bake, uncovered, about 15 minutes or until frittata sets. Stand 5 minutes before serving.

prep + cook time 35 minutes **serves** 4
nutritional count per serving 33.6g total fat (14.4g saturated fat); 1892kJ (452 cal); 20.3g carbohydrate; 31.9g protein; 5.6g fibre

tip You will need an ovenproof frying pan for this recipe. If necessary, protect the handle of the pan by wrapping it in foil.
serving suggestion Oak leaf and mixed herb salad with dijon vinaigrette (page 232).

note Beef stroganoff is a dish served in a sauce with sour cream. It originated in Russia in the 19th century and has since become popular around the world, with as many variations as there are countries that eat it. Here we've used pork instead of beef, but chicken may also be used.

pork stroganoff with parsley fettuccine

80g (2½ ounces) butter

1 medium brown onion (150g), cut into wedges

375g (12 ounces) sliced cup mushrooms

500g (1 pound) pork fillets, cut into 1cm (½-inch) thick strips

1½ teaspoons smoked paprika

1¼ cups (300g) sour cream

375g (12 ounces) fresh fettuccine pasta

½ cup firmly packed fresh flat-leaf parsley leaves

1 Melt half the butter in a medium saucepan over medium heat; cook the onion, stirring, until softened. Add the mushrooms; cook, stirring occasionally, about 5 minutes or until golden and liquid has evaporated.
2 Add pork and paprika; cook, stirring occasionally, for about 5 minutes or until browned lightly. Stir in sour cream; simmer, uncovered, about 5 minutes or until pork is tender.
3 Meanwhile, cook pasta in a large saucepan of boiling water until just tender; drain. Return pasta to pan with remaining butter and half the parsley; toss to combine.
4 Stir remaining parsley through the stroganoff; season to taste. Serve stroganoff with pasta.

prep + cook time 30 minutes **serves** 4
nutritional count per serving 48.9g total fat (30g saturated fat); 3821kJ (913 cal); 71.1g carbohydrate; 44.2g protein; 6.2g fibre

tip Toss the butter and parsley through the pasta as soon as it has been drained – the hot pasta will melt the butter.

READY IN
30
MINUTES

READY IN
30 MINUTES

tips Some butchers sell a pork and veal mixture. If it is not available as a mixture, buy half the amount as pork mince and half the amount as veal mince. Passata is available from most supermarkets. If you can't find it, use pureed canned tomatoes instead. You can freeze this dish in an airtight container for up to 1 month.

spanish spicy pork and veal meatballs

1½ tablespoons olive oil

1 medium brown onion (150g), chopped finely

3 sprigs fresh thyme

750g (1½ pounds) minced (ground) pork and veal mixture

1 cup (70g) fresh breadcrumbs

1 cup (100g) finely grated parmesan cheese

½ cup finely chopped fresh flat-leaf parsley

2 eggs

3 cloves garlic, crushed

2 teaspoons ground coriander

1 teaspoon each ground turmeric and nutmeg

½ teaspoon ground cinnamon

½ teaspoon dried chilli flakes

700ml (1½ pounds) passata

¼ cup loosely packed fresh flat-leaf parsley leaves

1 Heat 2 teaspoons of the oil in a deep, large frying pan over high heat; cook onion and thyme, stirring, until onion softens. Remove from pan.

2 Combine the pork and veal, breadcrumbs, cheese, parsley, eggs, garlic and spices in a large bowl; season. Using damp hands, roll the mixture into 12 balls.

3 Heat remaining oil in the same pan; cook the meatballs, turning, until well browned all over.

4 Return onion mixture to pan with passata; bring to the boil. Reduce heat; simmer, uncovered, about 5 minutes or until meatballs are cooked through. Sprinkle over extra parsley.

prep + cook time 30 minutes **serves** 4
nutritional count per serving 31.8g total fat (11.2g saturated fat); 2760kJ (659 cal); 28.3g carbohydrate; 61.7g protein; 8g fibre

serving suggestion Pilaf (see page 212).

READY IN
25
MINUTES

READY IN
15
MINUTES

pork and mango curry

blue cheese and salami omelette

pork 124

pork and mango curry

425g (13½ ounces) canned mango cheeks
400ml (12½ ounces) canned coconut cream (see tip)
2 tablespoons yellow curry paste
500g (1 pound) pork fillet, cut 1cm (½-inch) thick strips
½ cup (60g) frozen green peas
⅓ cup fresh mint leaves

1 Drain mango, reserving ¼ cup of the juice.
2 Heat a medium saucepan over medium heat. Spoon the thick cream layer off the top of the coconut cream into the pan; cook, stirring, until slightly golden. Stir in paste; cook until fragrant. Stir in remaining cream and reserved juice; bring to the boil. Reduce heat; simmer, uncovered, about 8 minutes or until sauce is reduced by about a third.
3 Stir pork into sauce; simmer, uncovered, about 10 minutes or until pork is tender. Add peas and mango; cook until heated through. Sprinkle with mint.

prep + cook time 25 minutes **serves** 4
nutritional count per serving 24.1g total fat (18.6g saturated fat); 1793kJ (428 cal); 19.7g carbohydrate; 31.7g protein; 4.4g fibre

tip You need to spoon the thick cream layer off the top of the coconut cream, so don't shake the can as the thick cream will separate from the liquid underneath. If you shake it, you have to wait until the liquid settles into layers again.
serving suggestion Serve with roti, or any flatbread you prefer, and mango pickles.

blue cheese and salami omelette

6 eggs, separated
50g (1½ ounces) butter
1 cup (200g) drained char-grilled capsicum (bell pepper) strips
50g (1½ ounces) shaved salami, torn
⅓ cup (80g) spinach and cashew parmesan dip
135g (4 ounces) blue cheese, crumbled

1 Preheat grill (broiler).
2 Beat egg whites in a large mixing bowl with an electric mixer until soft peaks form. Add yolks, beat to combine.
3 Melt butter in a deep 24cm (9½-inch) (base measurement) frying pan over medium heat. Pour in egg mixture; cook, uncovered, about 3 minutes or until omelette is almost set.
4 Sprinkle capsicum and salami over omelette; top with heaped teaspoons of dip and cheese. Place under hot grill for 2 minutes or until browned lightly and cooked through.
5 Serve omelette with toasted crusty bread, if you like.

prep + cook time 15 minutes **serves** 4
nutritional count per serving 45.7g total fat (19.8g saturated fat); 2226kJ (532 cal); 5.6g carbohydrate; 22.5g protein; 1.2g fibre

tip We used gorgonzola cheese, but any blue cheese will work well with this dish.

tip When stir-frying, make sure all the ingredients are ready to go, and that includes the water and sauces. Peel, chop and measure everything before heating the wok, making sure everything is cut to a uniform size and thickness to ensure even cooking. The preparation of a stir-fry actually takes longer than the cooking.

pork and brussels sprout stir-fry

⅓ cup (45g) slivered almonds

2 tablespoons peanut oil

1 large carrot (180g), cut into matchsticks

450g (14½ ounces) pork fillet, sliced thinly

500g (1 pound) brussels sprouts, halved

4 cloves garlic, sliced thickly

1 cup (250ml) water

2 tablespoons hoisin sauce

1 tablespoon soy sauce

1 Heat a large wok over high heat; stir-fry nuts until toasted. Remove from wok immediately.
2 Heat 2 teaspoons of the oil in same wok; stir-fry carrot until browned lightly and just tender. Remove from wok.
3 Heat 1 tablespoon of the remaining oil in wok; stir-fry pork, in batches, until browned and just cooked through.
4 Heat remaining oil in wok; stir-fry sprouts and garlic until golden. Add the water; simmer, loosely covered, until sprouts are just tender and water has evaporated. Return pork to wok with carrot and sauces; stir-fry until well coated and heated through.
5 Serve stir-fry sprinkled with nuts.

prep + cook time 20 minutes **serves** 4
nutritional count per serving 17.7g total fat (2.7g saturated fat); 1451kJ (347 cal); 9.5g carbohydrate; 33g protein; 9.9g fibre

serving suggestion Steamed rice.

READY IN
20
MINUTES

baked witlof with prosciutto

pork sausages with crispy potatoes and cabbage

pork 128

baked witlof with prosciutto

¼ cup (60ml) lemon juice

8 white witlof (belgian endive) (1.4kg)

40g (1½ ounces) butter

¼ cup (35g) plain (all-purpose) flour

2½ cups (625ml) milk

1 cup (125g) grated gruyère cheese

8 slices prosciutto (120g)

1 Bring a large saucepan of water to the boil; add the juice. Add witlof to pan; cook about 5 minutes or until tender.
2 Meanwhile, melt butter in a small saucepan over high heat. Add flour; cook, stirring, about 2 minutes or until it bubbles. Gradually whisk in milk until smooth; cook, stirring, until mixture boils and thickens. Add a third of the cheese, stirring, until melted.
3 Preheat oven to 220°C/425°F.
4 Drain witlof; cool under cold running water. Squeeze out excess moisture; pat dry with absorbent paper towel.
5 Wrap a strip of prosciutto around each witlof; place, in a single layer, in a 2.5-litre (10-cup) shallow ovenproof dish. Pour cheese sauce over witlof; sprinkle with remaining cheese.
6 Bake witlof 20 minutes or until golden and bubbly.

prep + cook time 30 minutes **serves** 4
nutritional count per serving 25.1g total fat (14.4g saturated fat); 1666kJ (398 cal); 17.6g carbohydrate; 23.8g protein; 5.8g fibre

tip Witlof is also known as belgian endive or chicory; is white (with pale green tips) or red, with tightly packed, cigar-shaped heads. When raw, it has a crunchy texture and a mildly bitter flavour. May also be eaten cooked, as in this recipe.
serving suggestion Baby spinach salad.

pork sausages with crispy potatoes and cabbage

750g (1½ pounds) desiree potatoes, cut into wedges

½ cup (125ml) olive oil

8 pork sausages (600g)

2 rindless bacon slices (130g), chopped coarsely

4 cloves garlic, crushed

½ small cabbage (600g), shredded finely

1 Microwave potatoes, covered, in a heatproof bowl, on HIGH (100%) for about 6 minutes or until just tender.
2 Heat 2 teaspoons of the oil in a large frying pan over high heat; cook sausages, turning occasionally, until browned and cooked through. Remove from pan; cover to keep warm.
3 Heat 2½ tablespoons of the remaining oil in a large saucepan over high heat; cook bacon, stirring, until browned. Add garlic, stirring, until fragrant. Add cabbage, reduce heat to low; cook, covered, about 5 minutes or until tender, stirring halfway through cooking time.
4 Meanwhile, heat remaining oil in same frying pan; cook potatoes, turning, about 10 minutes or until golden and crisp.
5 Serve sausages with cabbage and potatoes.

prep + cook time 30 minutes **serves** 4
nutritional count per serving 78.1g total fat (24.4g saturated fat); 4139kJ (989 cal); 31.7g carbohydrate; 36.8g protein; 9.8g fibre

tip Use a mandoline or V-slicer to finely shred the cabbage.

pork chops with blue-cheese sauce and cauliflower mash

1 medium cauliflower (1.5kg)

2 teaspoons olive oil

4 pork mid-loin chops (1.2kg)

1 cup (250ml) pouring cream

100g (3 ounces) gorgonzola cheese

½ cup (120g) ricotta cheese

¼ cup finely chopped fresh chives

1 Break cauliflower into florets. Place in a large bamboo steamer; steam, covered, over a large saucepan of boiling water about 12 minutes or until tender.
2 Meanwhile, heat oil in a large frying pan over high heat; cook pork for about 5 minutes each side or until cooked as desired. Cover to keep warm.
3 Discard oil from pan. Add cream and gorgonzola; cook, stirring, over medium heat until smooth. Bring to the boil; simmer about 2 minutes or until thickened.
4 Blend or process cauliflower and ricotta until almost smooth. Season to taste. Cover to keep warm.
5 Serve pork with cauliflower mash; drizzle over cheese sauce.

prep + cook time 30 minutes **serves** 4
nutritional count per serving 37.5g total fat (21.2g saturated fat); 2645kJ (632 cal); 8.5g carbohydrate; 57.8g protein; 9.2g fibre

serving suggestion Garlicky beans with pine nuts (page 225).

READY IN 30 MINUTES

READY IN
30
MINUTES

chinese pork and noodle soup

1.5 litres (6 cups) chicken stock

2 cups (500ml) water

8 slices dried shiitake mushrooms

4cm (1½-inch) piece fresh ginger (20g), cut into matchsticks

270g (8½ ounces) dried ramen noodles

500g (1 pound) baby pak choy, separated

¼ cup (60ml) soy sauce

⅓ cup (80ml) mirin

400g (12½ ounces) chinese barbecued pork, sliced thinly

4 green onions (scallions), sliced thinly

1 fresh long red chilli, sliced thinly

⅓ cup coarsely chopped fresh coriander (cilantro)

1 Place stock, the water, mushrooms and ginger in a large saucepan; bring to the boil. Reduce heat; simmer 10 minutes.
2 Meanwhile, cook noodles in a large saucepan of boiling water until tender; drain.
3 Return stock mixture to the boil; add pak choy, simmer until wilted. Stir in sauce and mirin.
4 Divide noodles among serving bowls; top with pork, onion, chilli and coriander. Pour over hot stock mixture.

prep + cook time 30 minutes **serves** 4
nutritional count per serving 17g total fat (6.3g saturated fat); 2651kJ (633 cal); 68g carbohydrate; 41.9g protein; 12.7g fibre

thai chilli pork

2 tablespoons peanut oil

4 cloves garlic, crushed

¼ cup (75g) thai red curry paste

500g (1 pound) minced (ground) pork

3 medium tomatoes (450g), chopped finely

2 tablespoons fish sauce

1 tablespoon lime juice

3 teaspoons brown sugar

¼ cup coarsely chopped fresh coriander (cilantro)

1 Heat oil in a wok over high heat; stir-fry garlic until fragrant. Add paste to wok, stirring, for 30 seconds. Add pork; stir-fry until changed in colour. Stir in tomato, then sauce, juice and sugar; stir-fry until well coated.
2 Sprinkle with coriander to serve.

prep + cook time 15 minutes **serves** 4
nutritional count per serving 26g total fat (6.4g saturated fat); 1632kJ (390 cal); 7.9g carbohydrate; 29.3g protein; 3.6g fibre

serving suggestion Steamed rice.

grilled miso pork cutlets

4 pork cutlets (940g)

1 clove garlic, crushed

1cm (½-inch) piece fresh ginger (5g), grated finely

2 green onions (scallions), chopped finely

2 tablespoons soy sauce

2 tablespoons sake

2 tablespoons mirin

2 tablespoons white miso

1 Combine ingredients in a shallow dish; rub marinade all over pork; stand 10 minutes. Drain pork over medium bowl; reserve marinade.
2 Cook pork on a heated oiled grill plate (or grill or barbecue), brushing with reserved marinade, for about 3 minutes each side or until cooked as desired.

prep + cook time 30 minutes **serves** 4
nutritional count per serving 23.8g total fat (8.2g saturated fat); 1725kJ (412 cal); 8.1g carbohydrate; 39.1g protein; 0.9g fibre

serving suggestion Steamed asian greens with char siu sauce (page 227) and jasmine rice.

READY IN 15 MINUTES

READY IN 30 MINUTES

thai chilli pork

grilled miso pork cutlets

READY IN
20
MINUTES

chorizo, tomato and rocket pasta salad

375g (12 ounces) fettuccine pasta

¼ cup (40g) pine nuts

1 cured chorizo sausage (170g), chopped coarsely

1 clove garlic, crushed

2 tablespoons extra virgin olive oil

1½ tablespoons lemon juice

250g (8-ounce) tub buffalo mozzarella cheese, drained, torn into bite-sized pieces

½ cup (75g) drained sun-dried tomatoes in oil, halved

100g (3 ounces) baby rocket leaves (arugula)

½ cup (40 g) flaked parmesan cheese

1 Cook pasta in a large saucepan of boiling water until just tender; drain.
2 Meanwhile, toast pine nuts in a dry medium frying pan, over high heat, stirring constantly, until golden brown. Remove from pan immediately.
3 Cook chorizo in same pan over high heat until browned. Drain on absorbent paper.
4 To make dressing, combine garlic, oil and juice in a small bowl; season to taste.
5 Place pasta, nuts and chorizo in a large bowl with dressing, mozzarella, tomato and rocket; toss gently to combine. Serve pasta sprinkled with parmesan.

prep + cook time 20 minutes **serves** 4
nutritional count per serving 36.9g total fat (11.5g saturated fat); 3187kJ (761 cal); 74.4g carbohydrate; 28.8g protein; 7.3g fibre

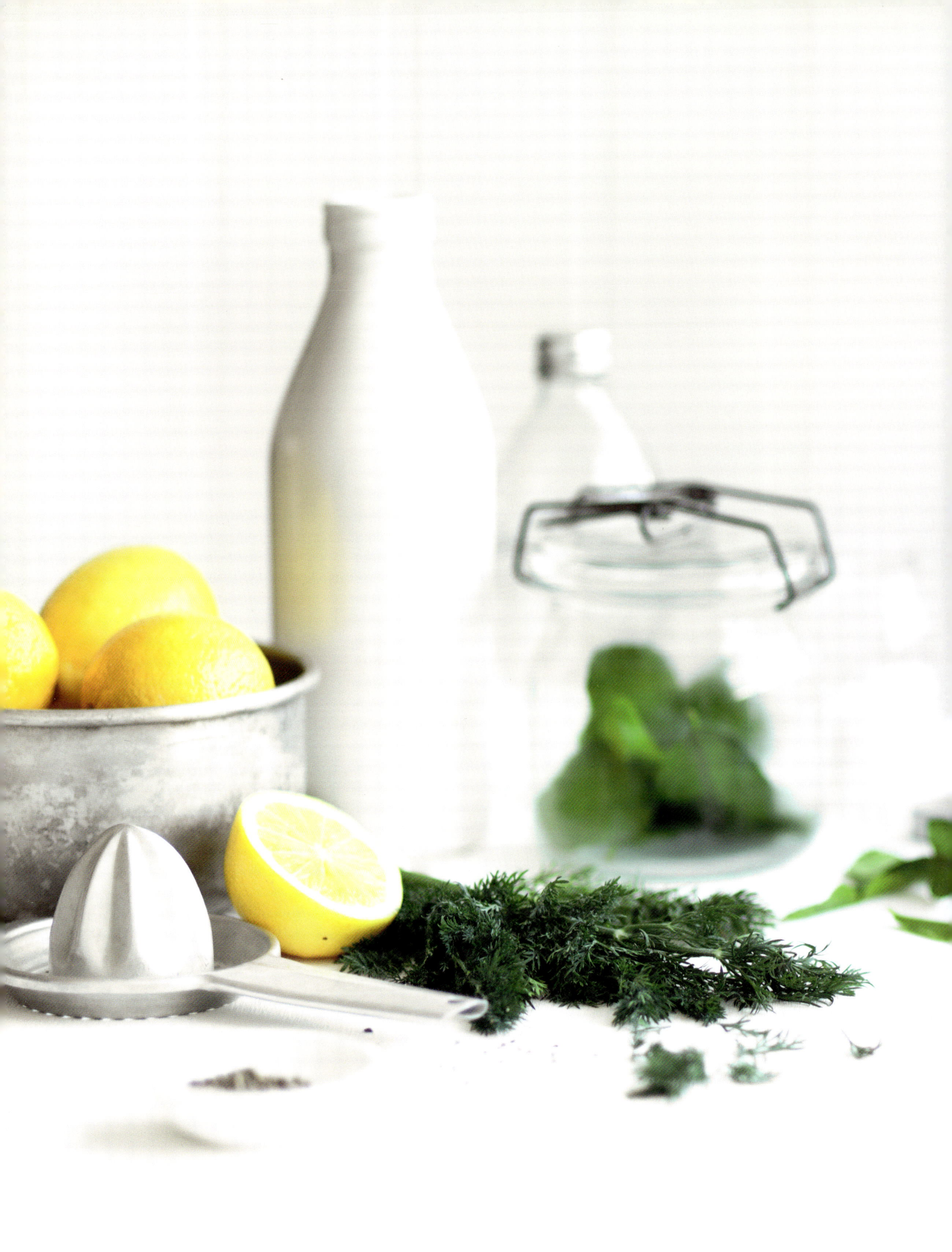

seafood

The fastest of all, seafood can be on the table in the time it takes to make a salad, boil the pasta, or cut the vegies for a stir-fry.

salmon and potato parcels

1 tablespoon olive oil

1 medium brown onion (150g), chopped finely

2 cloves garlic, crushed

400g (12½ ounces) canned crushed tomatoes

1 tablespoon each coarsely chopped fresh flat-leaf parsley and mint

4 baby new potatoes (chats) (160g), sliced thinly

4 x 220g (7-ounce) skinless salmon fillets

1 medium lemon (140g), sliced thinly

1 Preheat oven to 200°C/400°F.
2 Heat oil in a large frying pan; cook onion and garlic, stirring, until onion softens. Add tomatoes and herbs; bring to the boil. Reduce heat; simmer about 5 minutes or until mixture has thickened and reduced slightly. Season to taste.
3 Place potato, slightly overlapping, onto four 30cm x 40cm (12-inch x 16-inch) pieces of baking paper; top with salmon. Spoon tomato mixture over salmon; top with lemon. Fold paper to enclose fish.
4 Place parcels on a baking tray; bake about 15 minutes or until fish is cooked as desired. Serve fish in parcel.

prep + cook time 30 minutes **serves** 4
nutritional count per serving 28.4g total fat (6.9g saturated fat); 2222kJ (531 cal); 10.4g carbohydrate; 55.6g protein; 3.8g fibre

tip To fold the parcel, bring long sides to meet in the middle, fold over about 1cm (½-inch) folding all the way down. Then fold edges under to enclose.
serving suggestion Preserved lemon and olive couscous (page 208).

READY IN 30 MINUTES

READY IN
30
MINUTES

tip When buying prawns, look for brightly coloured, firm prawns with shiny shells and a pleasant fresh sea smell. As prawns are highly perishable when raw, some may be boiled at sea, as soon as they are caught, to preserve them. When cooking prawns, buy green (raw) prawns, as cooked ones will toughen if reheated.

sesame prawn and scallop stir-fry

440g (14 ounces) fresh egg noodles

2 tablespoons sesame seeds

500g (1 pound) uncooked king prawns (shrimp)

2 tablespoons sesame oil

300g (9½ ounces) scallops, roe removed

1 medium brown onion (150g), cut into thin wedges

1 medium carrot (120g), sliced thinly

¼ cup (95g) oyster sauce

1 tablespoon soy sauce

1 teaspoon fish sauce

150g (4½ ounces) baby pak choy, halved lengthways

4 green onions (scallions), sliced thinly diagonally

1 Place noodles in a medium heatproof bowl. Cover with boiling water; stand until noodles are tender. Drain.
2 Toast sesame seeds in a wok over high heat, stirring, until golden and fragrant. Remove from wok immediately.
3 Peel and devein prawns, leaving tails intact.
4 Heat half the oil in wok; stir-fry prawns and scallops, in batches, until prawns change colour. Remove from wok.
5 Heat remaining oil in wok; stir-fry brown onion and carrot until onion begins to soften. Add noodles and sauces; stir-fry 3 minutes. Return prawns and scallops to wok with pak choy and green onion; stir-fry until pak choy just begins to wilt. Serve stir-fry sprinkled with sesame seeds.

prep + cook time 30 minutes **serves** 4
nutritional count per serving 14.4g total fat (2.2g saturated fat); 1844kJ (440 cal); 37g carbohydrate; 37.1g protein; 6.1g fibre

creamy prawn and tomato spaghetti

750g (1½ pounds) cherry tomatoes, halved

1 fresh long red chilli, sliced thinly

2 cloves garlic, sliced thinly

3 sprigs fresh thyme

2 tablespoons olive oil

400g (12½ ounces) shelled uncooked medium king prawns (shrimp)

375g (12 ounces) spaghetti

½ cup (120g) crème fraîche

50g (1½ ounces) baby rocket leaves (arugula)

1 Preheat oven to 220°C/425°F.
2 Place tomato, chilli, garlic and thyme in a baking dish; drizzle with oil. Roast for 10 minutes. Add prawns to dish; roast for 5 minutes or until prawns are cooked through.
3 Meanwhile, cook pasta in a large saucepan of boiling water until just tender; drain. Return to pan.
4 Add prawn mixture with any juices to pasta; add crème fraîche and rocket to pan, toss gently to combine. Season to taste.

prep + cook time 25 minutes **serves** 4
nutritional count per serving 23.2g total fat (9.3g saturated fat); 2697kJ (644 cal); 71.5g carbohydrate; 33.2g protein; 7g fibre

prawn club sandwich with chips

800g (1½ pounds) frozen potato chips

4 rindless bacon slices (260g)

2 teaspoons olive oil

8 slices white sourdough bread (560g)

½ cup (150g) mayonnaise

1 small green oak leaf lettuce, leaves separated

2 medium tomatoes (300g), sliced thinly

500g (1 pound) shelled cooked tiger prawns (shrimp)

1 Preheat oven to 220°C/425°F. Cook chips according to packet directions.
2 Meanwhile, cut each bacon slice into three even pieces. Heat oil in a large frying pan over high heat; cook bacon about 5 minutes or until crisp. Drain on absorbent paper.
3 Toast bread until golden. Spread mayonnaise over toast slices; sandwich lettuce, tomato, bacon and prawns between toast slices. Serve with chips.

prep + cook time 35 minutes **serves** 4
nutritional count per serving 46.6g total fat (14.7g saturated fat); 4280kJ (1022 cal); 162g carbohydrate; 70.1g protein; 15.2g fibre

READY IN
25
MINUTES

READY IN
35
MINUTES

creamy prawn and tomato spaghetti

prawn club sandwich with chips

seafood 145

READY IN 30 MINUTES

note The original French salade niçoise was created with the finest local produce from Provence – vine-ripened tomatoes, piquant caperberries, tiny firm black olives, hand-picked baby beans and good-quality tuna.

niçoise salad

4 eggs

155g (5 ounces) green beans

4 x 250g (8-ounce) tuna steaks

1 small red onion (100g), cut into thin wedges

2 small vine-ripened tomatoes (180g), cut into wedges

1 cup (160g) caperberries

½ cup (90g) seeded black olives

90g (3 ounces) baby rocket leaves (arugula)

lemon dressing

2 tablespoons finely grated lemon rind

1 tablespoon lemon juice

¼ cup (60ml) olive oil

1 Place eggs in a small saucepan, cover with water; bring to the boil, simmer 5 minutes. Drain; cool, then peel. Cut into quarters.
2 Meanwhile, boil, steam or microwave beans until just tender, refresh under cold water. Cool.
3 Make lemon dressing.
4 Cook tuna on a heated oiled grill plate (or grill or barbecue) for 2 minutes each side or until cooked as desired.
5 Arrange eggs and beans between serving plates with onion, tomato, caperberries and olives. Top with tuna and rocket; drizzle with dressing.
lemon dressing Combine ingredients in a screw-top jar; shake well.

prep + cook time 30 minutes **serves** 4
nutritional count per serving 26.5g total fat (4.8g saturated fat); 2457kJ (587 cal); 6.2g carbohydrate; 78.3g protein; 3.8g fibre

barbecued chilli prawns with green mango and coconut salad

1 fresh long red chilli, chopped finely

1 tablespoon finely grated lime rind

1 tablespoon lime juice

2 tablespoons char siu sauce

1 tablespoon honey

2 tablespoons olive oil

1kg (2 pounds) uncooked king prawns (shrimp)

green mango and coconut salad

200g (6½ ounces) vermicelli (glass) noodles

½ cup (25g) flaked coconut

1 medium green mango (350g), shredded

1 fresh long red chilli, sliced thinly

⅓ cup (50g) roasted cashew nuts

90g (3 ounces) baby rocket leaves (arugula)

1 cup loosely packed coriander leaves (cilantro)

¼ cup (60ml) olive oil

2 tablespoons lemon juice

1 Combine chilli, rind, juice, sauce, honey, oil and prawns in a large bowl, stir to coat prawns in mixture. Cover; refrigerate until required.
2 Make green mango and coconut salad.
3 Cook prawns on a heated oiled grill plate (or grill or barbecue) about 6 minutes or until prawns just change in colour and are cooked through.
4 Serve prawns with salad.
green mango and coconut salad Place noodles in a medium heatproof bowl; cover with boiling water, stand 3 minutes or until noodles are tender. Drain. Cook coconut in a dry frying pan, stirring frequently, over medium heat, about 2 minutes or until browned lightly. Place noodles and coconut in a large bowl with remaining ingredients; toss gently to combine.

prep + cook time 30 minutes **serves** 4
nutritional count per serving 34.2g total fat (8.3g saturated fat); 2360kJ (564 cal); 32.7g carbohydrate; 30.5g protein; 3.9g fibre

tip Use a V-slicer or mandoline to thinly shred the mango.

READY IN
30
MINUTES

READY IN
25
MINUTES

READY IN
20
MINUTES

salmon pies

asian mussels

salmon pies

4 sheets puff pastry

4 x 220g (7-ounce) skinless salmon fillets

4 green onions (scallions), sliced thinly

1 tablespoon finely chopped fresh dill

1 tablespoon rinsed, drained baby capers

1 egg, beaten lightly

1 Preheat oven to 180°C/350°F. Oil and line a large baking tray with baking paper.
2 Place pastry sheets on a clean flat surface. Place one salmon fillet in the centre of each pastry sheet; season. Top salmon with onion, dill and capers. Brush egg lightly over pastry edges.
3 Working with one pastry sheet at a time, fold opposite sides of the pastry over the salmon. Fold other sides over to completely enclose salmon and form a parcel. Repeat with remaining pastry.
4 Place parcels, seam-side down, on baking tray. Using a sharp knife, make three diagonal slits across the top of each parcel (without cutting through pastry). Brush top of pastry with egg.
5 Bake parcels about 15 minutes or until golden.

prep + cook time 25 minutes **makes** 4
nutritional count per pie 69.8g total fat (32.2g saturated fat); 5043kJ (1204 cal); 76.8g carbohydrate; 66.8g protein; 3.1g fibre

serving suggestion Tomato and herb salad (page 231).

asian mussels

3 cups (750ml) water

1½ cups (300g) white rice

⅓ cup (80ml) japanese soy sauce

⅓ cup (80ml) mirin

⅓ cup (80ml) lime juice

1 tablespoon peanut oil

2 fresh long red chillies, sliced thinly

2 cloves garlic, crushed

5cm (2-inch) piece fresh ginger (20g), grated finely

4 green onions (scallions), sliced thinly

2kg (4 pounds) pot-ready mussels

½ cup loosely packed fresh coriander leaves (cilantro)

1 lime, cut into wedges

1 Bring the water to the boil in a large saucepan. Rinse rice under cold running water until the water runs clear; drain. Add rice to the boiling water; cook, covered, over very low heat, for 10 minutes. Remove from heat; stand 10 minutes. Fluff with a fork.
2 Combine sauce, mirin and lime juice in a small jug.
3 Heat oil in a large saucepan; cook chilli, garlic and ginger, stirring, until fragrant. Add sauce mixture; bring to the boil. Stir in onion and mussels; cook, covered, for about 5 minutes or until mussels open.
4 Sprinkle mussels with coriander; accompany with rice and lime wedges.

prep + cook time 20 minutes **serves** 6
nutritional count per serving 5.6g total fat (1.3g saturated fat); 1418kJ (339 cal); 50.3g carbohydrate; 17.6g protein; 1g fibre

tips Pot-ready mussels come in 1kg (2-pound) bags. They have been scrubbed and bearded and are ready to cook. Some mussels may not open up during cooking; in fact, some will not open after excessive cooking. Don't discard these, just open with a knife or cook a little more, if you like.

tips Hot smoked salmon is available from major supermarkets. Use a mixture of fresh herbs, such as dill, parsley, basil, chives, mint, oregano or marjoram. If you don't have a frying pan with an ovenproof handle, wrap the handle in two layers of foil, this will prevent the handle from burning while under the grill.

hot smoked salmon and goat's cheese frittata

20g (¾ ounce) butter

1 large brown onion (200g), sliced thinly

2 cloves garlic, sliced thinly

8 eggs

⅔ cup (160ml) pouring cream

½ cup chopped fresh mixed herbs

⅔ cup (50g) finely grated parmesan cheese

340g (11 ounces) asparagus, trimmed

150g (4½ ounces) hot smoked salmon

75g (2½ ounces) goat's cheese

30g (1 ounce) beetroot leaves

1½ tablespoons fresh dill sprigs

2 teaspoons olive oil

1 Preheat grill (broiler).
2 Melt butter in a medium 22cm (8¾-inch) (base measurement) ovenproof frying pan over medium heat; cook onion and garlic, stirring, until onion softens.
3 Meanwhile, whisk eggs, cream, herbs and half the parmesan in a large jug.
4 Cut asparagus diagonally into 4cm (1½-inch) lengths, add to pan; cook, over high heat, stirring, about 5 minutes or until tender. Add salmon and egg mixture to pan. Reduce heat to medium-low; cook about 8 minutes or until set around the edges. Crumble goat's cheese on top; sprinkle with remaining parmesan. Place frying pan under grill; cook for 5 minutes or until golden and set.
5 Toss beetroot leaves, dill and oil in a small bowl.
6 Serve frittata, cut into wedges, topped with beetroot leaves.

prep + cook time 30 minutes **serves** 4
nutritional count per serving 41.3g total fat (21.4g saturated fat); 2219kJ (530 cal); 4.3g carbohydrate; 35g protein; 2.8g fibre

READY IN 30 MINUTES

READY IN
30
MINUTES

note The colour of olives depends on their level of ripeness. Green olives are picked before fully ripened, while black olives are those picked when ripe. Green olives, therefore, are generally denser, firmer and more bitter than black ones.

smoky prawn and chorizo stew

1 tablespoon olive oil

1 large red onion (300g), chopped finely

3 cloves garlic, crushed

45g (1½ ounces) drained canned anchovies, chopped finely

1 cured chorizo sausage (170g), sliced thinly

1 large red capsicum (bell pepper) (350g), chopped coarsely

2 teaspoons paprika

pinch saffron

400g (12½ ounces) canned diced tomatoes

½ cup (125ml) water

1kg (2 pounds) shelled uncooked medium king prawns (shrimp)

½ cup (60g) drained halved green olives

2 tablespoons small fresh flat-leaf parsley leaves

1 Heat oil in a large saucepan over high heat; cook onion, garlic, anchovy and chorizo, stirring, until onion softens. Add capsicum, paprika and saffron; cook, stirring, about 1 minute or until fragrant. Add tomatoes and the water; bring to the boil. Reduce heat; simmer, uncovered about 10 minutes or until capsicum is tender and sauce thickens.
2 Add prawns; cook, stirring occasionally, about 5 minutes or until prawns are cooked through.
3 Serve stew topped with olives and parsley.

prep + cook time 30 minutes **serves** 4
nutritional count per serving 17.9g total fat (4.4g saturated fat); 1997kJ (477 cal); 10.4g carbohydrate; 64.9g protein; 5.9g fibre

serving suggestion Slices of grilled ciabatta or wood-fired bread.

char-grilled thai squid salad

1kg (2 pounds) cleaned squid hoods

2 cloves garlic, crushed

1 tablespoon peanut oil

170g (5½ ounces) asparagus, trimmed

175g (5½ ounces) broccolini, trimmed

200g (6½ ounces) sugar snap peas

1 cup loosely packed fresh mint leaves

½ cup loosely packed fresh coriander leaves (cilantro)

2 limes, cut into cheeks

chilli dressing

1 fresh long red chilli, chopped finely

⅓ cup (80ml) lime juice

1 tablespoon peanut oil

2 teaspoons fish sauce

2 teaspoons brown sugar

1 Cut squid down the centre to open out. Score the inside, without cutting all the way through, in a diagonal criss-cross pattern; cut into thick strips. Combine squid, garlic and oil in a large bowl; season.
2 Cook squid on a heated oiled grill plate (or grill or barbecue), turning occasionally, until cooked through.
3 Meanwhile, make chilli dressing.
4 Boil, steam or microwave asparagus, broccolini and sugar snap peas, separately, until tender.
5 Place squid and vegetables in a large bowl with herbs and dressing; toss gently to combine. Serve salad with lime cheeks.
chilli dressing Combine ingredients in a screw-top jar; shake well.

prep + cook time 30 minutes **serves** 4
nutritional count per serving 12.6g total fat (2.7g saturated fat); 1406kJ (336 cal); 4.9g carbohydrate; 46.8g protein; 5.1g fibre

READY IN 30 MINUTES

curly fettuccine with smoked salmon

500g (1 pound) curly fettuccine pasta

1½ cups (360g) crème fraîche

⅓ cup (80ml) dry white wine

1 tablespoon rinsed, drained baby capers

2 teaspoons finely grated lemon rind

⅓ cup (80ml) lemon juice

200g (6½ ounces) hot smoked salmon, flaked

½ cup shredded fresh basil leaves

1 Cook pasta in a large saucepan of boiling water until just tender; drain, reserving 1½ cups of the cooking liquid. Return pasta to pan.
2 Meanwhile, combine crème fraîche, wine, capers and rind in a small bowl.
3 Add crème fraîche mixture to pasta with juice and reserved cooking liquid; stir over medium heat until combined. Add salmon and basil; cook, stirring, until hot. Season to taste.

prep + cook time 20 minutes **serves** 6
nutritional count per serving 27.4g total fat (15.6g saturated fat); 2442kJ (583 cal); 61.1g carbohydrate; 20g protein; 2.9g fibre

tip Hot smoked salmon is available from major supermarkets.
serving suggestion Tomato and herb salad (page 231).

prawn caesar salad

4 eggs

2 tablespoons olive oil

4 slices stale sourdough bread (125g), torn into chunks

4 slices prosciutto (60g), halved lengthways

450g (14½ ounces) shelled cooked small prawns (shrimp)

½ cup (125ml) caesar salad dressing

2 tablespoons lemon juice

2 baby cos (romaine) lettuce, leaves separated

1 Place eggs in a small saucepan, cover with water; bring to the boil, simmer 5 minutes. Drain; cool, then peel. Cut into halves.
2 Meanwhile, heat oil in a medium frying pan over high heat; cook bread and prosciutto, stirring, until browned and crispy. Transfer to a large bowl.
3 Cook prawns with half the dressing in same pan, stirring, until just warm. Add prawns to bread mixture with juice; toss gently to combine. Season to taste.
4 Serve prawn mixture on lettuce with eggs; drizzle with remaining dressing.

prep + cook time 20 minutes **serves** 4
nutritional count per serving 29g total fat (6.3g saturated fat); 2046kJ (489 cal); 16.6g carbohydrate; 39.2g protein; 3.1g fibre

curly fettuccine with smoked salmon

prawn caesar salad

seafood 159

baked snapper

tarragon mussels

seafood 160

baked snapper

500g (1 pound) baby new potatoes (chats)

2 medium tomatoes (300g)

3 medium red onions (510g), sliced thinly

1 fresh long red chilli, sliced thinly

2 tablespoons shredded fresh basil

⅓ cup (80ml) olive oil

2 x 500g (1-pound) whole cleaned snapper

1 Preheat oven to 220°C/425°F.
2 Boil, steam or microwave potatoes until just cooked; drain.
3 Meanwhile, seed tomatoes; slice into thin strips. Place half the onion and half the tomato in a large baking dish; top with chilli and half the basil, drizzle with 1 tablespoon of the oil.
4 Season fish; place on onion and tomato in baking dish. Top with remaining onion, tomato and basil; add potatoes and drizzle with remaining oil.
5 Roast about 12 minutes or until fish is just cooked through.

prep + cook time 30 minutes **serves** 4
nutritional count per serving 20g total fat (3.4g saturated fat); 1570kJ (375 cal); 21.6g carbohydrate; 24.6g protein; 5.2g fibre

tip To check if the fish is cooked, insert a knife into the thickest part of the flesh; the flesh should pierce easily with no resistance to the knife. The flesh will also have turned opaque.

tarragon mussels

1kg (2 pounds) frozen fries

60g (2 ounces) butter

1 small brown onion (100g), chopped finely

1 clove garlic, crushed

⅓ cup (80ml) dry white wine

2kg (4 pounds) pot-ready mussels

1 tablespoon finely chopped fresh tarragon

1 Preheat oven to 240°C/475°F. Cook fries according to directions on packet.
2 Meanwhile, melt butter in a large saucepan over medium heat; cook onion, stirring, until softened. Stir in garlic; cook until fragrant. Add wine; bring to the boil.
3 Add mussels to pan; simmer, covered, until mussels open. Stir in tarragon; season. Serve mussels with fries; accompany with crusty bread, if you like.

prep + cook time 30 minutes **serves** 4
nutritional count per serving 35.7g total fat (19.4g saturated fat); 2097kJ (501 cal); 116.9g carbohydrate; 32.3g protein; 12.1g fibre

tip Pot-ready mussels come in 1kg (2-pound) bags. They have been scrubbed and bearded and are ready to cook. Some mussels may not open during cooking – some will not open after excessive cooking. You do not have to discard these; just cook a little longer, or carefully prise the shell open with a knife.

tip If you are unable to buy tuna pasta bake sauce you can use any commercially-made white sauce.

tuna macaroni

300g (9½ ounces) macaroni

1¾ cups (350g) roasted red capsicum (bell pepper) strips in oil, drained

425g (13½ ounces) canned tuna in spring water, drained

425g (13½ ounces) canned asparagus spears, drained

2¼ cups (540g) tuna pasta bake sauce

1½ cups (180g) coarsely grated cheddar cheese

1 cup (75g) panko (japanese) breadcrumbs

2 tablespoons torn fresh flat-leaf parsley

1 Preheat oven to 200°C/400°F. Oil 6 x 1½-cup (375ml) ovenproof dishes.
2 Cook pasta in a large saucepan of boiling water until just tender; drain.
3 Combine pasta, capsicum, tuna, asparagus and sauce in a large bowl; spoon mixture equally into dishes. Sprinkle with combined cheese and breadcrumbs. Bake about 10 minutes or until browned and heated through. Sprinkle with parsley.

prep + cook time 25 minutes **serves** 6
nutritional count per serving 20.7g total fat (9.5g saturated fat); 2442kJ (583 cal); 58g carbohydrate; 38.2g protein; 4.4g fibre

serving suggestion Oak leaf and mixed herb salad with dijon vinaigrette (page 232).

READY IN
25
MINUTES

READY IN
20 MINUTES

tips Coriander is one of the few fresh herbs to be sold with its root attached. It should be readily available from greengrocers. Asian greengrocers will certainly stock it. Remove the salmon from the pan when it is still a little rare in the centre as it will continue to cook on standing.

salmon with nam jim on cucumber salad

1 tablespoon vegetable oil

4 x 180g (6-ounce) salmon fillets

2 lebanese cucumbers (260g)

2 red radishes (140g), sliced thinly

¼ cup lightly packed fresh coriander leaves (cilantro)

nam jim

1 clove garlic

3 fresh long red chillies, seeded, chopped coarsely

3 shallots (75g), chopped coarsely

2cm (¾-inch) piece fresh ginger (10g), chopped coarsely

2 fresh coriander (cilantro) roots, trimmed

2 tablespoons fish sauce

2 tablespoons brown sugar

¼ cup (60ml) lime juice

¼ cup lightly packed fresh coriander (cilantro) leaves

1 Make nam jim.
2 Rub oil over salmon; season. Heat a medium frying pan over high heat; cook salmon, skin-side down, for about 5 minutes or until skin is crisp, pressing down with a spatula to prevent curling. Turn salmon, cook a further 1 minute or until cooked as desired.
3 Meanwhile, using a vegetables peeler, cut cucumber lengthways into ribbons. Combine cucumber, radish and coriander in a small bowl.
4 Serve salmon with cucumber salad and nam jim.
nam jim Blend or process ingredients until almost smooth. Season to taste with extra fish sauce, sugar or juice, as required.

prep + cook time 20 minutes **serves** 4
nutritional count per serving 24.2g total fat (5.6g saturated fat); 1854kJ (443 cal); 10g carbohydrate; 45.6g protein; 2.8g fibre

serving suggestion Jasmine rice or steamed ginger rice (page 214).

korma prawn curry

1 tablespoon vegetable oil

2 medium brown onions (300g), chopped finely

3 cloves garlic, crushed

¼ cup (75g) korma curry paste

1 cup (250ml) water

700g (1½ pounds) frozen prawn cutlets

2 medium zucchini (300g), chopped coarsely

1 cup (120g) frozen peas

¼ cup (60ml) pouring cream

1 fresh long red chilli, sliced thinly

1 cup fresh coriander leaves (cilantro)

1 Heat oil in a large saucepan over medium heat; cook onion, stirring, about 5 minutes or until golden. Add garlic; cook, stirring, until fragrant. Stir in paste; cook, stirring, 2 minutes.
2 Stir in the water; bring to the boil. Add prawns; cover, bring to the boil. Add zucchini; simmer, covered, about 6 minutes or until prawns are pink and zucchini is just tender. Stir in peas and cream.
3 Serve curry topped with chilli and coriander.

prep + cook time 30 minutes **serves** 4
nutritional count per serving 17.8g total fat (4.8g saturated fat); 1552kJ (371 cal); 8.7g carbohydrate; 40.8g protein; 5.2g fibre

tip Purchase frozen fresh prawn cutlets not crumbed prawn cutlets; they come in 1kg (2-pound) 'ready-to-cook' packets. If you can't find them, use frozen uncooked prawns, instead.
serving suggestion Steamed basmati rice.

warm potato and smoked trout salad

750g (1½ pounds) kipfler (fingerling) potatoes, unpeeled

1 tablespoon dijon mustard

2 tablespoons red wine vinegar

1 tablespoon finely chopped fresh dill

¼ cup (60ml) olive oil

300g (9½ ounces) whole hot smoked trout

1 stalk celery (150g), trimmed, sliced thinly

1 shallot (25g), sliced thinly

150g (4½ ounces) mixed salad leaves

1 tablespoon rinsed, drained baby capers

1 Place potatoes in a medium saucepan; cover with water, season with salt. Bring to the boil; boil about 15 minutes or until tender. Drain. Cut into 2cm (¾-inch) slices.
2 Meanwhile, whisk mustard, vinegar and dill in a small bowl; gradually whisk in oil. Season to taste.
3 Place warm potatoes in a large serving bowl with mustard dressing; toss gently to coat.
4 Discard skin and bones from trout; flake into large chunks. Add trout to potatoes with celery, shallot, salad leaves and capers; toss gently to combine.

prep + cook time 30 minutes **serves** 4
nutritional count per serving 18.3g total fat (3.2g saturated fat); 1467kJ (351 cal); 25g carbohydrate; 18.6g protein; 4.7g fibre

korma prawn curry

warm potato and smoked trout salad

seafood 167

READY IN
30
MINUTES

fish chowder with garlic and chive rolls

2 medium potatoes (400g)

500g (1 pound) firm white fish fillets

80g (2½ ounces) butter, softened

2 cloves garlic, crushed

¼ cup finely chopped fresh chives

4 small bread (dinner) rolls (360g)

4 rindless bacon slices (260g), chopped coarsely

1 medium brown onion (150g), chopped coarsely

2 tablespoons plain (all-purpose) flour

2 cups (500ml) milk

3 cups (750ml) fish stock

420g (13½ ounces) canned corn kernels, rinsed, drained

170g (5½ ounces) asparagus, trimmed, chopped coarsely

1 Preheat oven to 180°C/350°F.
2 Cut potatoes into 2cm (¾-inch) pieces. Cut fish into 3cm (1¼-inch) pieces.
3 Combine half the butter, half the garlic and 1 tablespoon of the chives in a small bowl. Make three cuts vertically in top of rolls, without cutting all the way through. Spread butter mixture into cuts. Wrap rolls in foil; bake about 8 minutes or until heated through.
4 Meanwhile, cook bacon in a large saucepan over high heat on stove top, stirring occasionally, until browned lightly. Add onion; cook, stirring occasionally, until onion softens. Add remaining garlic; cook, stirring, until fragrant.
5 Melt remaining butter in same pan, add flour; cook, stirring, until bubbling. Gradually stir in milk, then stock; cook, stirring, until mixture boils and thickens. Stir in potato and corn; simmer, covered, about 12 minutes or until potato is tender, stirring occasionally. Add fish and asparagus; simmer, uncovered, about 2 minutes or until just cooked through. Season to taste; stir in remaining chives. Serve with rolls.

prep + cook time 30 minutes **serves** 4
nutritional count per serving 34.8g total fat (17.7g saturated fat); 3725kJ (890 cal); 84g carbohydrate; 55.9g protein; 9.4g fibre

tips You can use steamed fresh clams instead of the fish. Chicken or vegetable stock is also fine to use in this recipe.

tips You'll need about four large limes for this recipe. Shelled prawns are available in fish shops and frozen in supermarkets.

hot and sour prawn noodle soup

1½ cups (375ml) fish stock

1.5 litres (6 cups) water

3 kaffir lime leaves, torn in half

10cm (4-inch) stick fresh lemon grass (20g), halved lengthways

3cm (1¼-inch) piece fresh ginger (15g), sliced thinly

⅓ cup (75g) tom yum paste

2 tablespoons fish sauce

½ cup (125ml) lime juice

⅓ cup (75g) firmly packed brown sugar

200g (6½ ounces) rice stick noodles

400g (12½ ounces) baby buk choy, quartered

200g (6½ ounces) button mushrooms, halved

400g (12½ ounces) shelled uncooked medium king prawns (shrimp)

3 fresh small red thai (serrano) chillies, sliced thinly

¼ cup lightly packed fresh coriander leaves (cilantro)

1 Place stock, the water, lime leaves, lemon grass and ginger in a large saucepan; bring to the boil. Reduce heat; simmer, covered, 5 minutes. Remove lime leaves, lemon grass and ginger with a slotted spoon. Stir in paste; return to the boil. Stir in sauce, juice and sugar.
2 Meanwhile, place noodles in a large heatproof bowl; cover with boiling water, stand 5 minutes or until tender. Drain.
3 Add buk choy to the stock mixture with mushrooms, prawns and chilli; simmer, uncovered, until prawns are just cooked through. Stir in noodles; simmer, uncovered, until hot. Season to taste.
4 Serve soup with coriander, and a squeeze of lime, if you like.

prep + cook time 25 minutes **serves** 4
nutritional count per serving 3.2g total fat (0.5g saturated fat); 1201kJ (287 cal); 32.9g carbohydrate; 28.2g protein; 5.4g fibre

READY IN
25
MINUTES

READY IN
30
MINUTES

tips Larger supermarkets stock ready-mashed potato; you will find it either in the freezer or refrigerated sections. If you don't have a V-slicer or mandoline, use a large sharp knife to slice the vegetables.

salmon patties with fennel salad

415g (13 ounces) canned red salmon
475g (15 ounces) tub plain mashed potato
4 green onions (scallions), chopped finely
1 egg, beaten lightly
½ cup (35g) panko (japanese) breadcrumbs
¼ cup coarsely chopped fresh dill
¾ cup (45g) panko (japanese) breadcrumbs, extra
2 tablespoons olive oil
⅓ cup (80ml) light thickened (heavy) cream
1 egg yolk
2 tablespoons lemon juice

fennel, cabbage and radish salad
1 small fennel bulb (200g)
¼ medium savoy cabbage (375g)
8 red radishes (280g)
1 tablespoon extra virgin olive oil
2 teaspoons lemon juice
1 teaspoon wholegrain mustard

1 Drain salmon; remove skin and bones. Flake salmon into a large bowl.
2 Drain any liquid from potato. Add potato to bowl with onion, egg, breadcrumbs and 2 tablespoons of the dill, season; mix well. Using damp hands, shape the mixture into 12 patties. Coat patties in extra breadcrumbs; pressing lightly. Refrigerate 10 minutes.
3 Meanwhile, make fennel, cabbage and radish salad.
4 Heat oil in a large frying pan over medium heat; cook patties until browned on both sides and heated through.
5 Heat cream in a small saucepan over low heat until warm. Whisk in egg yolk and juice until sauce thickens; stir in remaining dill, season to taste.
6 Serve patties on salad, drizzled with sauce; top with reserved fennel tips.
fennel, cabbage and radish salad Reserve fennel tips for serving. Using a mandoline or V-slicer, finely slice fennel, cabbage and radishes. Place vegetables in a medium bowl with combined remaining ingredients. Season to taste.

prep + cook time 30 minutes **serves** 4
nutritional count per serving 25.4g total fat (6.4g saturated fat); 1760kJ (420 cal); 27.5g carbohydrate; 24.7g protein; 6.7g fibre

crispy parmesan fish fillets

2 slices multigrain bread (90g)

¼ cup (40g) pine nuts

1 cup loosely packed fresh flat-leaf parsley

¼ cup (20g) finely grated parmesan cheese

40g (1½ ounces) butter, melted

4 x 210g (6½ ounces) skinless white fish fillets

1 lemon, cut into wedges

1 Preheat oven to 180°C/350°F. Grease and line a large baking tray with baking paper.
2 Blend or process bread, nuts, parsley and cheese until fine. Add butter; process until combined.
3 Place fish on baking tray; season. Evenly press breadcrumb mixture over top of fillets. Bake about 15 minutes or until topping is crisp and fish is cooked through. Accompany with lemon wedges.

prep + cook time 25 minutes **serves** 4
nutritional count per serving 33.2g total fat (7.3g saturated fat); 2923kJ (698 cal); 42.7g carbohydrate; 54.3g protein; 4.4g fibre

serving suggestion Leafy green salad.

tip When buying firm white fish fillets, blue eye, bream, flathead, swordfish, ling, whiting, jewfish, sea perch or snapper are all good choices. Check for any small pieces of bone in the fillets and use tweezers to remove them.

READY IN 25 MINUTES

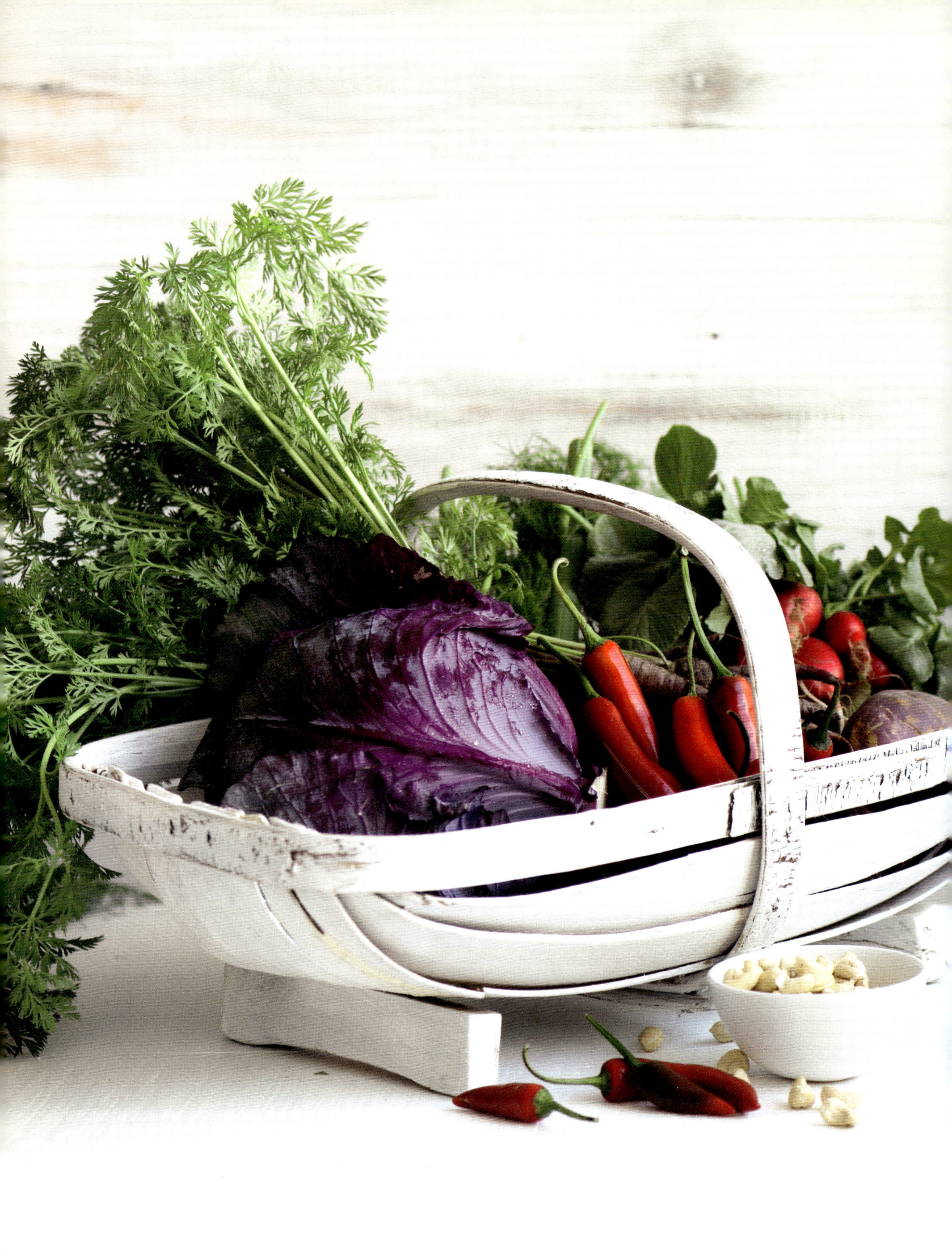

vegetarian

Not just lentils – these pastas, frittatas, soups, vegetable bakes, salads and curries are just as delicious without the meat.

note Artichoke hearts are the tender centres of the globe artichoke, which has tough petal-like leaves that are edible, in part, when cooked. (It is actually a large flower bud of a member of the thistle family.) Artichoke hearts are available fresh from the plant, or purchased in brine, either canned or in glass jars.

spaghetti with artichokes, asparagus and peas

375g (12 ounces) spaghetti

2 tablespoons olive oil

170g (5½ ounces) asparagus, halved on the diagonal

2 cloves garlic, crushed

1 cup (120g) frozen peas

280g (9 ounces) bottled artichoke hearts in brine, drained, halved

1 cup (240g) ricotta cheese, crumbled

1 Cook pasta in a large saucepan of boiling water until just tender; drain.
2 Meanwhile, heat oil in a large frying pan; cook asparagus and garlic, stirring, about 2 minutes or until asparagus is just tender. Add peas and artichokes; cook for 2 minutes.
3 Add drained spaghetti to asparagus mixture; stir until heated through. Serve pasta topped with ricotta.

prep + cook time 25 minutes **serves** 4
nutritional count per serving 15.5g total fat (4.8g saturated fat); 1156kJ (276 cal); 62.4g carbohydrate; 10.1g protein; 9.8g fibre

READY IN 25 MINUTES

cauliflower and cheese pasta bake

wild mushroom and green onion frittata

cauliflower and cheese pasta bake

250g (8 ounce) packet spiral (corkscrew) pasta

30g (1 ounce) butter

2 tablespoons plain (all-purpose) flour

2 cups (500ml) milk

1½ cups (150g) coarsely grated mozzarella cheese

2 tablespoons coarsely chopped fresh flat-leaf parsley

500g (1 pound) frozen cauliflower florets

1 egg, beaten lightly

¼ cup (20g) panko (japanese) breadcrumbs

½ teaspoon ground nutmeg

1 Preheat grill (broiler). Oil a 2-litre (8-cup) ovenproof dish.
2 Cook pasta in a large saucepan of boiling water until just tender; drain.
3 Meanwhile, to make cheese sauce, melt butter in a medium saucepan, add flour; cook, stirring, until bubbling. Gradually stir in milk; cook, stirring, until mixture boils and thickens. Remove from heat; stir in 1 cup of the cheese, and the parsley.
4 Combine pasta, cheese sauce and cauliflower in a large bowl; stir in egg. Spoon mixture into dish, top with combined breadcrumbs and remaining cheese; sprinkle with nutmeg.
5 Place under hot grill about 10 minutes or until golden brown.

prep + cook time 25 minutes **serves** 4
nutritional count per serving 22g total fat (12.9g saturated fat); 2361kJ (564 cal); 59.8g carbohydrate; 27.7g protein; 4g fibre

serving suggestion Oak leaf and mixed herb salad with dijon vinaigrette (page 232).

wild mushroom and green onion frittata

10 eggs

½ cup (120g) sour cream

½ cup (40g) finely grated parmesan cheese

1 tablespoon olive oil

3 green onions (scallions), chopped on the diagonal

1 clove garlic, crushed

200g (6½ ounces) mixed mushrooms, sliced thinly

1 Preheat oven to 220°C/425°F.
2 Whisk eggs, cream and cheese in a medium bowl until combined.
3 Heat oil in a 19cm (7¾-inch) (base measurement) ovenproof frying pan; cook onion and garlic, stirring, until garlic is fragrant. Remove pan from heat; stir in mushrooms until combined. Pour egg mixture over mushroom mixture. Cook over medium heat until sides begin to set.
4 Transfer frittata to oven; bake about 20 minutes or until centre of frittata is set and top is browned lightly.
5 Cut frittata into wedges to serve.

prep + cook time 30 minutes **serves** 4
nutritional count per serving 34.4g total fat (14.9g saturated fat); 1745kJ (417 cal); 2.3g carbohydrate; 24.9g protein; 1g fibre

tips You need an ovenproof frying pan for this recipe as it goes into the oven; or cover the handle with a few layers of foil to protect it from the heat.
We used a mix of oyster, shiitake, swiss and portobello mushrooms.
serving suggestion Baby spinach and parmesan salad (page 233).

white minestrone

1 tablespoon extra virgin olive oil

1 large brown onion (200g), sliced thinly

2 cloves garlic, crushed

1 large fennel bulb (550g), sliced thinly, reserve fronds

¼ small savoy cabbage (300g), sliced thinly

3 cups (750ml) vegetable stock

3 cups (750ml) water

2 cups (160g) dried fusilli pasta

400g (12½ ounces) canned cannellini beans, rinsed, drained

½ cup (60g) frozen peas

1 cup (80g) finely grated parmesan cheese

⅓ cup (90g) basil pesto

¼ cup (25g) flaked parmesan cheese

1 Heat oil in a large saucepan over high heat; cook onion, garlic and fennel, stirring, until softened. Add cabbage, stock and the water; bring to the boil. Reduce heat; simmer, uncovered, 10 minutes. Add pasta; cook, stirring occasionally, until tender.
2 Add beans, peas and grated cheese to pan; cook, stirring occasionally, about 5 minutes or until heated through.
3 Serve minestrone topped with pesto, flaked cheese and reserved fennel fronds.

prep + cook time 30 minutes **serves** 4
nutritional count per serving 23.7g total fat (7.8g saturated fat); 2277kJ (544 cal); 53.3g carbohydrate; 26.1g protein; 7.1g fibre

tip Fusilli are long, thick corkscrew (spiral) shaped pasta.

kumara potato jackets

4 small kumara (orange sweet potato) (1kg)

2 eggs, beaten lightly

⅔ cup roughly chopped fresh chives

150g (4½ ounces) soft goat's cheese

1 Preheat oven to 200°C/400°F. Line a baking tray with foil.
2 Scrub kumara; pierce all over with a fork. Wrap in plastic wrap; cook in a microwave oven on HIGH (100%) for about 8 minutes or until tender. Cool 5 minutes; unwrap.
3 Cut a 2cm (¾-inch) deep incision, lengthways from one end of the kumara to the other. Using a tea towel, gently squeeze the base of the kumara to open the top. Scoop two thirds of flesh into a small bowl. Repeat with remaining kumara.
4 Add egg and half the chives to kumara flesh; stir to combine, season. Divide mixture between kumara; top with crumbled cheese. Place on baking tray.
5 Bake stuffed kumara about 5 minutes or until golden brown. Sprinkle with remaining chives.

prep + cook time 25 minutes **serves** 4
nutritional count per serving 10.5g total fat (6.1g saturated fat); 1285kJ (307 cal); 35.8g carbohydrate; 15.1g protein; 4.8g fibre

serving suggestion Baby spinach and parmesan salad (page 233).

READY IN
30
MINUTES

READY IN
25
MINUTES

white minestrone

kumara potato jackets

vegetarian 183

falafel with eggplant puree and tomato salsa

2 medium eggplants (460g)

450g (14½ ounces) packaged falafel

2 cloves garlic, quartered

2 tablespoons tahini

¾ cup (210g) greek-style yogurt

2 tablespoons lemon juice

3 medium tomatoes (450g), chopped finely

¼ cup finely chopped fresh mint

2 tablespoons finely chopped fresh flat-leaf parsley

250g (8 ounces) rocket leaves (arugula)

2 tablespoons olive oil

1 Preheat oven to 200°C/400°F.
2 Cut eggplant in half lengthways. Using a small knife, cut a criss-cross pattern over cut sides of eggplant. Cook eggplant on a heated oiled grill plate (or grill or barbecue), cut-side down, until tender and soft. Cool slightly.
3 Meanwhile, cook falafel in oven according to directions on packet.
4 Using a spoon, scrape eggplant flesh from skin. Discard skin. Blend or process flesh with garlic, tahini, yogurt and juice until almost smooth; season to taste.
5 To make salsa, combine tomato, mint and parsley in a medium bowl; season to taste.
6 Serve falafel with eggplant puree, rocket and salsa; drizzle with oil. Accompany with grilled flatbread, if you like.

prep + cook time 30 minutes **serves** 4
nutritional count per serving 35.7g total fat (5.5g saturated fat); 2309kJ (552 cal); 30.7g carbohydrate; 18.1g protein; 19.5g fibre

vegetarian 184

READY IN 30 MINUTES

mixed mushrooms on creamy polenta

3 cups (750ml) water

1½ cups (375ml) vegetable stock

1½ cups (375ml) milk

1½ cups (250g) polenta

⅓ cup (25g) finely grated parmesan cheese

1 tablespoon olive oil

50g (1½ ounces) butter

600g (1¼ pounds) mixed mushrooms, sliced thinly

2 cloves garlic, crushed

1 tablespoon fresh thyme leaves

2 tablespoons coarsely chopped fresh chives

1 Place the water, stock and milk in a large saucepan; bring to the boil. Gradually add polenta; stir constantly, over low heat, about 10 minutes or until polenta thickens. Stir in cheese; season to taste.
2 Heat oil and butter in a large frying pan; cook mushrooms, garlic and thyme, stirring occasionally, until browned. Season to taste.
3 Serve polenta topped with mushroom mixture; sprinkle with chives, and extra fresh thyme, if you like.

prep + cook time 20 minutes **serves** 4
nutritional count per serving 22.3g total fat (11.2g saturated fat); 1293kJ (309 cal); 52.5g carbohydrate; 16.6g protein; 4.6g fibre

tip We used equal quantities of button, swiss brown, shiitake, oyster and enoki mushrooms. If using enoki mushrooms, add these at the end of cooking as they do not need as much cooking as the other mushroom varieties.

roast pumpkin and chickpea salad

1.3kg (2¾ pounds) butternut pumpkin, peeled, chopped coarsely

1 tablespoon olive oil

¼ cup (35g) unsalted pistachios

400g (12½ ounces) canned chickpeas (garbanzo beans), rinsed, drained

1 small red onion (100g), sliced thinly

150g (4½ ounces) baby spinach leaves

1 tablespoon coarsely chopped fresh chives

100g (3 ounces) fetta cheese, crumbled

preserved lemon vinaigrette

1 clove garlic, crushed

2 teaspoons finely chopped preserved lemon rind

2 tablespoons olive oil

1½ tablespoons white wine vinegar

1 Preheat oven to 200°C/400°F.
2 Combine pumpkin and oil in a large baking dish; season. Roast about 15 minutes or until tender.
3 Meanwhile, place nuts on a baking tray; roast, in oven, about 3 minutes or until golden. Remove from tray immediately.
4 Make preserved lemon vinaigrette.
5 Place pumpkin in a large bowl with chickpeas, onion, spinach leaves and vinaigrette; toss gently to combine. Serve salad sprinkled with nuts, chives and cheese.
preserved lemon vinaigrette Combine ingredients in a screw-top jar; shake well.

prep + cook time 30 minutes **serves** 4
nutritional count per serving 35g total fat (8.1g saturated fat); 2231kJ (533 cal); 34.1g carbohydrate; 15.5g protein; 12.4g fibre

tip To use preserved lemon rind, remove and discard the pulp, squeeze juice from rind, rinse rind well and chop finely.

READY IN
20
MINUTES

READY IN
30
MINUTES

mixed mushrooms on creamy polenta

roast pumpkin and chickpea salad

vegetarian 187

READY IN 30 MINUTES

note Paneer (or panir), most often used in curried dishes, originates from northern India; it is a fresh un-ripened cow's-milk cheese that is similar to pressed ricotta. It has no added salt and does not melt at normal cooking temperatures. Available in many major supermarkets (near the fetta and haloumi) and from Indian food stores; fetta or haloumi can replace paneer, but the results won't be the same.

paneer and vegetable curry

2 tablespoons peanut oil

1 large brown onion (200g), sliced thinly

2 cloves garlic, sliced thinly

4cm (1½-inch) piece fresh ginger (20g), grated

⅓ cup (100g) balti curry paste

400g (12½ ounces) canned chickpeas (garbanzo beans), rinsed, drained

400g (12½ ounces) canned diced tomatoes

½ cup (125ml) water

400g (12½ ounce) paneer cheese

150g (4½ ounces) green beans, halved lengthways

¼ cup (60ml) pouring cream

½ cup fresh coriander leaves (cilantro)

1 Heat half the oil in a large saucepan over high heat; cook onion, garlic and ginger, stirring, until onion softens. Add curry paste; cook, stirring, about 1 minute or until fragrant.
2 Add chickpeas, tomatoes and the water; bring to the boil. Reduce heat; simmer, covered, for 5 minutes.
3 Meanwhile, cut cheese into 3cm (1¼-inch) pieces. Heat remaining oil in a large frying pan over medium heat; cook cheese, turning, until browned all over. Remove from pan; cool then roughly crumble cheese.
4 Add beans and cream to curry; cook about 5 minutes or until beans are tender. Stir in half the cheese; cook until heated through. Serve sprinkled with coriander and remaining cheese. Accompany with warmed chapatti or naan bread, if you like.

prep + cook time 30 minutes **serves** 4
nutritional count per serving 30.3g total fat (10.2g saturated fat); 2433kJ (581 cal); 19.8g carbohydrate; 23.3g protein; 9.1g fibre

tip Paneer is a type of cheese popular in India. It is available from major supermarkets and Indian food stores.

ricotta and spinach agnolotti

625g (1¼ pounds) fresh ricotta and spinach agnolotti

50g (1½ ounces) butter

500g (1 pound) silver beet (swiss chard), trimmed, shredded finely

1½ teaspoons ground cinnamon

1kg (2 pounds) canned pumpkin soup

½ cup (125ml) pouring cream

100g (3 ounces) white mould cheese, crumbled

1 Cook agnolotti in a large saucepan of boiling water until tender; drain.
2 Melt butter in same cleaned pan over medium heat; cook silver beet, covered, about 5 minutes or until slightly wilted. Add cinnamon; cook, stirring, until fragrant.
3 Add soup to pan, bring to the boil; boil for 2 minutes. Add cream and agnolotti; stirring until well combined and heated through. Season to taste. Stand 5 minutes before serving.
4 Sprinkle agnolotti with cheese; serve with extra cinnamon, if you like.

prep + cook time 25 minutes **serves** 6
nutritional count per serving 31.3g total fat (19.6g saturated fat); 2465kJ (589 cal); 55.7g carbohydrate; 18.9g protein; 5.2g fibre

tips We used agnolotti, but any vegetarian-style pasta will work well in this dish. We used a white cheese from the Castello range; it has a mild, slightly tart, flavour. As it matures, it becomes creamier, and develops a fuller flavour.

curried vegetable and lentil soup

1 litre (4 cups) vegetable stock

1 litre (4 cups) water

500g (1 pound) butternut pumpkin, peeled, chopped finely

2 teaspoons olive oil

1 medium brown onion (170g), chopped finely

1 large clove garlic, crushed

1 medium carrot (120g), chopped finely

1 stalk celery (150g), trimmed, chopped finely

3 teaspoons curry powder

1 cup (120g) frozen peas

400g (12½ ounces) canned brown lentils, rinsed, drained

¼ cup (60ml) lemon juice

¼ cup fresh coriander leaves (cilantro)

1 Place stock, the water and pumpkin in a medium saucepan; cover, bring to the boil. Reduce heat; simmer, uncovered, about 5 minutes or until pumpkin is nearly tender.
2 Meanwhile, heat oil in a large saucepan over high heat; cook onion, garlic, carrot and celery, stirring, until softened. Add curry powder; stir until fragrant. Add pumpkin mixture and peas to pan; simmer about 10 minutes or until vegetables are tender. Stir in lentils and juice.
3 Serve curry sprinkled with coriander. Accompany with crusty bread, if you like.

prep + cook time 30 minutes **serves** 6
nutritional count per serving 2.7g total fat (0.5g saturated fat); 530kJ (127 cal); 15.3g carbohydrate; 7.2g protein; 6.7g fibre

ricotta and spinach agnolotti

curried vegetable and lentil soup

vegetarian 191

READY IN 30 MINUTES

root vegetable soup with cheesy brioche toasts

2 medium carrots (240g), chopped coarsely

2 stalks celery (300g), trimmed, chopped coarsely

1 large parsnip (350g), chopped coarsely

2 medium potatoes (400g), chopped coarsely

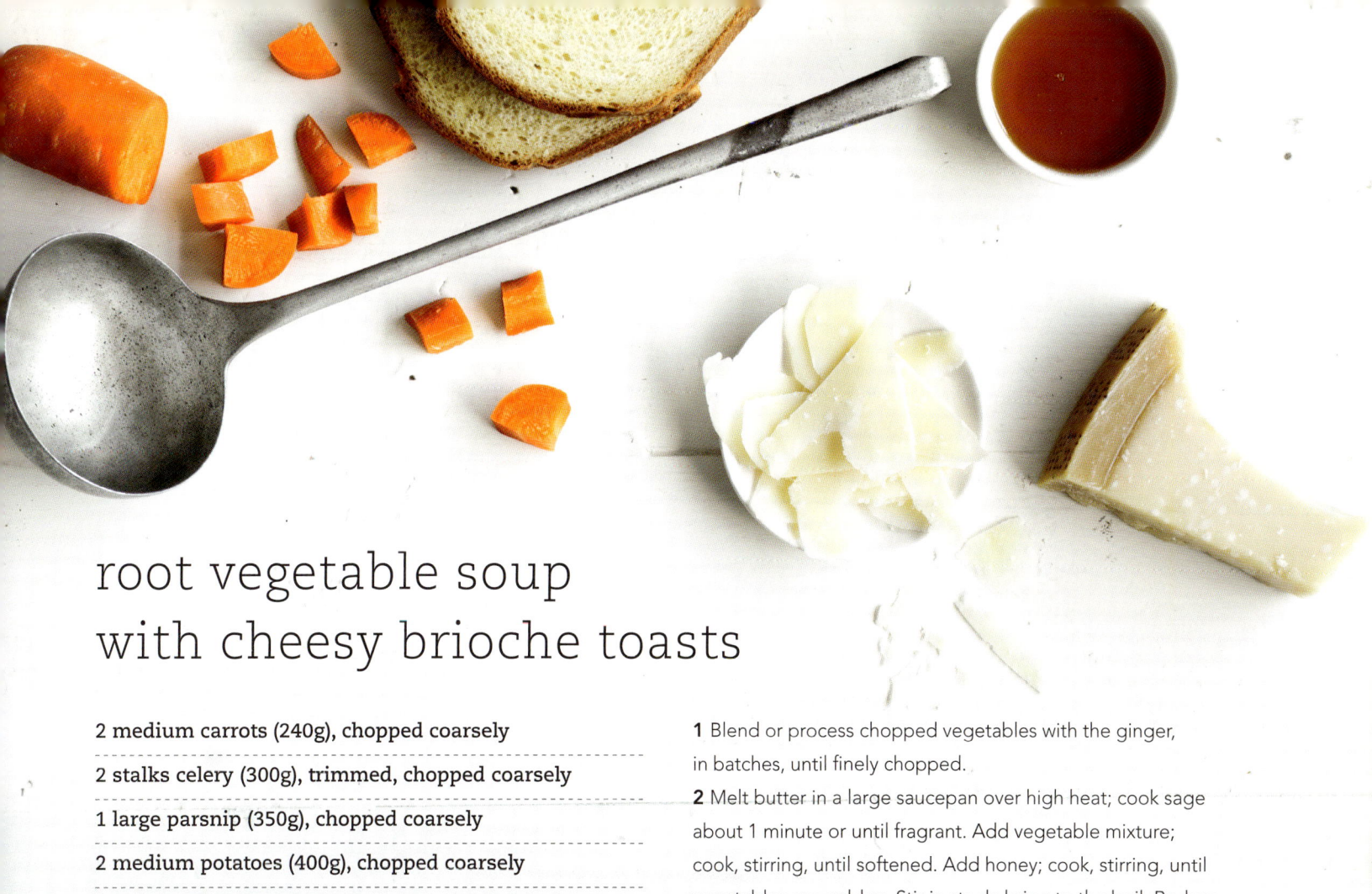

4cm (1½-inch) piece fresh ginger (30g), chopped coarsely

50g (1½ ounces) butter

¼ cup loosely packed fresh sage leaves

2 teaspoons honey

3½ cups (875ml) chicken stock

½ cup (125ml) pouring cream

2 tablespoons finely chopped fresh chives

cheesy brioche toasts

1 small brioche (100g)

⅓ cup (25g) flaked parmesan cheese

14 fresh sage leaves

1 Blend or process chopped vegetables with the ginger, in batches, until finely chopped.
2 Melt butter in a large saucepan over high heat; cook sage about 1 minute or until fragrant. Add vegetable mixture; cook, stirring, until softened. Add honey; cook, stirring, until vegetables are golden. Stir in stock; bring to the boil. Reduce heat; simmer, covered, 15 minutes or until vegetables are soft. Cool 10 minutes.
3 Meanwhile, make cheesy brioche toasts.
4 Blend or process soup, in batches, until smooth. Return to pan; stir in cream until heated through. Season to taste.
5 Sprinkle soup with chives; drizzle over a little extra cream, if you like. Serve with cheesy brioche toasts.
cheesy brioche toasts Preheat grill (broiler). Thinly slice brioche into 14 slices. Toast one side of brioche slices under hot grill; turn, sprinkle with cheese, top with one sage leaf. Grill until browned lightly.

prep + cook time 30 minutes **serves** 4
nutritional count per serving 25.8g total fat (15.7g saturated fat); 2231kJ (533 cal); 59.7g carbohydrate; 12g protein; 8.3g fibre

note The mushrooms and spinach will produce a lot of liquid while resting. Squeeze out and discard the excess liquid from the mushrooms, garlic and spinach before adding to the egg mixture.

mushroom, potato and spinach tortilla

500g (1 pound) desiree potatoes, cut into cubes

2 tablespoons olive oil

200g (6½ ounces) button mushrooms, quartered

3 cloves garlic, crushed

120g (4 ounces) baby spinach leaves

8 eggs

½ cup (125ml) pouring cream

¼ cup (20g) finely grated parmesan cheese

1 Preheat grill (broiler).
2 Boil, steam or microwave potatoes until just tender; drain.
3 Meanwhile, heat half the oil in a large ovenproof frying pan over high heat; cook mushrooms, stirring, until golden. Add garlic; cook, stirring, until fragrant. Add spinach leaves; cook, stirring, until wilted. Remove from pan; squeeze excess moisture from mixture.
4 Heat remaining oil in same cleaned pan over high heat; cook potatoes, stirring, until golden and tender.
5 Meanwhile, whisk eggs in a large bowl until combined. Whisk in cream; stir in cheese and mushroom mixture. Season.
6 Pour the egg mixture over potatoes; cook, over medium heat, about 6 minutes (pull in the edges to help the egg cook) or until the base and side are set. Place under hot grill; cook for about 8 minutes or until just set.

prep + cook time 30 minutes **serves** 4
nutritional count per serving 22.2g total fat (9.7g saturated fat); 1253kJ (299 cal); 15.1g carbohydrate; 8.1g protein; 3.8g fibre

serving suggestion Leafy green salad or trimmed watercress.

READY IN
30
MINUTES

bean and basil soup

spicy tofu stir-fry

vegetarian 196

bean and basil soup

1 tablespoon extra virgin olive oil

1 medium brown onion (150g), chopped finely

3 cloves garlic, crushed

1 litre (4 cups) vegetable stock

1 cup (250ml) water

800g (1½ pounds) canned butter beans, rinsed, drained

250g (8 ounces) green beans, halved

2 large zucchini (300g), halved lengthways, sliced thickly crossways

½ cup (40g) shaved parmesan cheese

2 tablespoons bottled basil pesto

1 Heat oil in a large saucepan over medium heat; cook, onion, stirring, until softened. Stir in garlic; cook until fragrant. Stir in stock and the water; bring to the boil. Add butter beans; simmer, covered, 10 minutes.
2 Add green beans and zucchini to soup; simmer, covered, 5 minutes or until vegetables are just tender, season. Sprinkle soup with cheese; accompany with pesto.

prep + cook time 30 minutes **serves** 4
nutritional count per serving 13.7g total fat (3.9g saturated fat); 1275kJ (305 cal); 24.3g carbohydrate; 17.4g protein; 12.8g fibre

spicy tofu stir-fry

320g (10 ounces) hard tofu

2 teaspoons peanut oil

300g (9½ ounces) snake beans, cut into 5cm (2-inch) pieces

1 medium red capsicum (bell pepper) (200g), sliced thinly

peanut oil, extra, for deep-frying

¼ cup (35g) cornflour (cornstarch)

1 teaspoon chinese five spice powder

3 cloves garlic, crushed

4cm (1½-inch) piece fresh ginger (20g), grated finely

1 fresh long green chilli, chopped finely

2 green onions (scallions), chopped finely

1 tablespoon soy sauce

1 Drain tofu between sheets of absorbent paper.
2 Heat oil in a wok over high heat; stir-fry beans 3 minutes. Add capsicum; stir-fry about 3 minutes or until just tender. Remove from wok.
3 Heat enough extra oil in wok to come halfway up the side. Cut tofu into 16 cubes. Toss tofu into combined cornflour and five-spice until well coated; shake off excess. Deep-fry tofu, in batches, about 2 minutes or until golden and crisp. Remove with slotted spoon; drain on absorbent paper. Discard oil.
4 Stir-fry garlic, ginger, chilli and onion in wok over medium heat until fragrant. Return beans and capsicum to wok with soy sauce and tofu; toss until heated through.

prep + cook time 30 minutes **serves** 4
nutritional count per serving 12.6g total fat (2g saturated fat); 836kJ (200 cal); 12.3g carbohydrate; 12.7g protein; 9.4g fibre

tip We used hard (stir-frying) tofu; you can substitute firm tofu, if you prefer.
serving suggestion Steamed rice.

READY IN
35
MINUTES

tips You can use prepared peeled, chopped pumpkin to save time; it's available from most greengrocers and major supermarkets. Paneer is a type of cheese popular in India. It is available from major supermarkets and Indian food stores. Omit the chilli if you like.

curried pumpkin crêpes

½ medium butternut pumpkin (1kg), peeled, cut into 2.5cm (1-inch) pieces

1 cup (270g) cashew masala simmer sauce

400g (12½ ounces) canned brown lentils, rinsed, drained

100g (3 ounces) baby spinach leaves

8 savoury crêpes (400g)

1 cup (250ml) coconut cream

100g (3 ounces) paneer cheese, crumbled

3 large roma (egg) tomatoes (270g), chopped finely

1 small red onion (100g), chopped finely

2 tablespoons coarsely chopped fresh coriander (cilantro)

1 fresh long red chilli, sliced thinly

1 Preheat oven to 220°C/425°F.

2 Boil, steam or microwave pumpkin until tender; drain.

3 Heat sauce in a large frying pan until fragrant. Add pumpkin; cook, stirring, until broken down and hot. Add lentils and spinach leaves; cook, stirring, until heated through. Season to taste.

4 Place crêpes on board; spoon pumpkin mixture along the centre of each crêpe. Roll to enclose filling. Place crêpes, seam-side down, just touching, in a shallow 20cm x 32cm (8-inch x 12¾-inch) ovenproof dish. Drizzle coconut cream over crêpes; sprinkle with cheese.

5 Bake crêpes about 15 minutes or until heated through and browned lightly.

6 Meanwhile, combine tomato, onion, coriander and chilli in a medium bowl; season to taste.

7 Serve crêpes with tomato mixture.

prep + cook time 35 minutes **serves** 4
nutritional count per serving 29.1g total fat (18.3g saturated fat); 2741kJ (655 cal); 66.8g carbohydrate; 18.7g protein; 10.4g fibre

spicy eggplant with soft-boiled eggs and labne

2 tablespoons extra virgin olive oil

1 large eggplant (500g), cut into 2.5cm (1-inch) pieces

1 large brown onion (200g), chopped coarsely

1 fresh long red chilli, sliced thinly

2 cloves garlic, crushed

2 teaspoons ground cumin

1 teaspoon ground coriander

400g (12½ ounces) canned chickpeas (garbanzo beans), rinsed, drained

800g (1½ pounds) canned diced tomatoes

1 cup (250ml) vegetable stock

8 eggs

1 loaf turkish bread (430g), sliced thickly

2 teaspoons extra virgin olive oil, extra

80g (2½ ounces) baby spinach leaves

160g (5 ounces) drained labne

½ teaspoon sumac

1 Heat half the oil in a large saucepan over high heat; cook eggplant, stirring, until browned and tender. Remove from pan.
2 Heat remaining oil in same pan; cook onion and chilli, stirring, until soft. Add garlic, cumin and coriander; cook, stirring, until fragrant.
3 Return eggplant to pan with chickpeas, undrained tomatoes and stock; simmer, covered, 15 minutes. Season to taste.
4 Meanwhile, place eggs in another large saucepan; cover with cold water. Cover pan with lid; bring to the boil. Boil eggs, uncovered, 2 minutes. Drain immediately. Run eggs under cold water until cool enough to handle. Peel eggs.
5 Preheat grill (broiler).
6 Place bread on oven tray; brush with extra oil. Place under hot grill until lightly toasted both sides.
7 Cut eggs in half. Divide eggplant mixture between shallow serving bowls; top with spinach leaves, eggs and labne. Sprinkle with sumac; serve with toasted bread.

prep + cook time 30 minutes **serves** 4
nutritional count per serving 36.5g total fat (11.7g saturated fat); 3417kJ (816 cal); 71.3g carbohydrate; 43.6g protein; 13.7g fibre

READY IN 30 MINUTES

tip Labne is a soft cheese originating from the Middle-East. It's made from strained yogurt, and is available from major supermarkets and Middle-Eastern food shops.

READY IN
30 MINUTES

tips Alternatively, the frittata can be made in a 24cm/9½-inch non-stick ovenproof frying pan, cooked, covered, over a medium-low heat for 12 minutes, then transferred to a hot grill (broiler) for 3 minutes or until browned lightly. You will need an ovenproof frying pan if it goes under the grill (or cover the handle with a few layers of foil to protect it from the heat). You can use other short pasta, such as macaroni or penne.

three-cheese pasta frittata

125g (4 ounces) farfalle (bow tie) pasta

1 tablespoon olive oil

4 green onions (scallions), chopped coarsely

¾ cup (150g) drained char-grilled capsicum (bell pepper), chopped coarsely

2 cloves garlic, crushed

8 drained cherry bocconcini cheese (85g)

100g (3 ounces) drained persian fetta cheese

¼ cup lightly packed fresh basil leaves

8 eggs

½ cup (40g) grated parmesan cheese

1 Preheat oven to 220°C/425°F.
2 Cook pasta in a large saucepan of boiling water for 2 minutes less than the packet instructions indicate; drain.
3 Meanwhile, heat oil in a medium frying pan over medium heat heat; cook onion and capsicum, stirring, for 3 minutes or until softened. Add garlic; cook, stirring, until fragrant. Add pasta; toss until well combined. Spread mixture evenly into a greased 24cm (9½-inch) round ovenproof pie dish. Top with bocconcini and crumbled fetta. Tear any large basil leaves in half; press half of the basil leaves into the mixture.
4 Whisk eggs in a large jug; season. Stir in parmesan. Pour egg mixture over pasta mixture; bake 20 minutes or until set and top is golden.
5 Scatter with remaining basil leaves. Cut into wedges to serve.

prep + cook time 30 minutes **serves** 4
nutritional count per serving 29.4g total fat (13.6g saturated fat); 2089kJ (499 cal); 24.3g carbohydrate; 33.1g protein; 2.6g fibre

serving suggestion Tomato and herb salad (page 231).

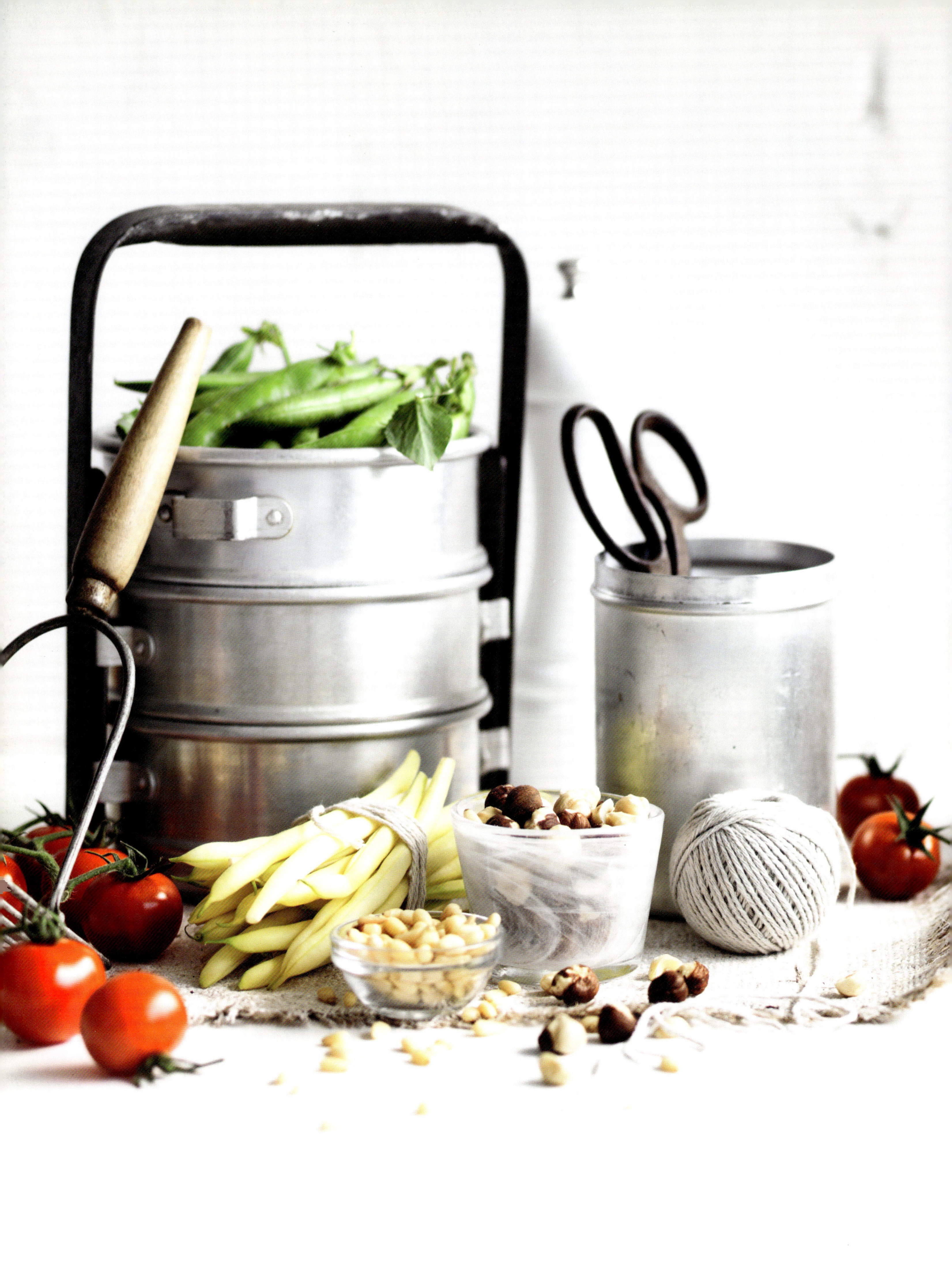

sides

What turns a steak into a meal – a side, of course. Make your choice of polenta, couscous, mash, salads, rice and vegies.

soft polenta

Combine 3 cups milk and 2 cups chicken stock in a large saucepan; bring to the boil. Gradually add 2 cups polenta to liquid, stirring constantly. Reduce heat; simmer, stirring, about 10 minutes or until polenta thickens. Add 1 cup milk and ¼ cup finely grated parmesan cheese; stir until cheese melts.

prep + cook time 20 minutes **serves** 6
nutritional count per serving 12.1g total fat (7.5g saturated fat); 621kJ (148 cal); 23.9g carbohydrate; 9.4g protein; 0.7g fibre

cheesy pesto polenta

To make pesto, blend or process 2 tablespoons each of finely grated parmesan, pine nuts and olive oil, 1 clove crushed garlic and 1 cup firmly packed basil leaves until mixture forms a paste. Combine 2⅓ cups water and 2⅓ cups milk in a large saucepan; bring to the boil. Gradually sprinkle 1 cup polenta over milk mixture; cook, stirring, until polenta thickens slightly. Reduce heat; simmer, uncovered, about 20 minutes or until polenta is thickened, stirring constantly. Stir in ½ cup finely grated parmesan cheese, 30g butter (1 ounce) and the pesto. Season to taste.

prep + cook time 35 minutes **serves** 4
nutritional count per serving 31.2g total fat (12.3g saturated fat); 1594kJ (381 cal); 39.2g carbohydrate; 15.5g protein; 2.2g fibre

tip If you don't want to make your own pesto, use 95g (3 ounces) of the store-bought variety.

green onion couscous

Bring 1½ cups chicken stock to the boil in a large saucepan. Remove from heat; add 1½ cups couscous and 25g (¾ ounce) butter; stir to combine. Cover; stand for about 5 minutes or until liquid is absorbed, fluffing with fork occasionally. Stir in 3 thinly sliced green onions.

prep + cook time 10 minutes **serves** 4
nutritional count per serving 6g total fat (3.6g saturated fat); 1404kJ (336 cal); 58.5g carbohydrate; 10.8g protein; 0.8g fibre

caprese salad

Overlap 3 thinly sliced large roma (egg) tomatoes and 310g (10 ounces) thinly sliced bocconcini cheese on serving platter. Drizzle with 2 tablespoons olive oil; sprinkle with ¼ cup firmly packed torn fresh basil leaves.

prep time 15 minutes **serves** 4
nutritional count per serving 20.6g total fat (8.8g saturated fat); 1028kJ (246 cal); 1.6g carbohydrate; 13.6g protein; 1.1g fibre

lemon pistachio couscous

Combine 1 cup couscous, ¾ cup boiling water, 2 teaspoons finely grated lemon rind and ¼ cup lemon juice in a medium heatproof bowl. Cover; stand about 5 minutes or until liquid is absorbed, fluffing with fork occasionally. Meanwhile, dry-fry ½ cup pistachios in a heated small frying pan until fragrant; remove nuts from pan, chop coarsely. Heat 2 teaspoons olive oil in same pan, add 1 clove crushed garlic and 1 finely chopped small red onion; cook, stirring, until onion softens. Fluff the couscous then stir nuts, onion mixture and ½ cup shredded fresh mint through couscous.

prep + cook time 15 minutes **serves** 4
nutritional count per serving 10.6g total fat (1.3g saturated fat); 1321kJ (316 cal); 42.8g carbohydrate; 10.2g protein; 2.8g fibre

preserved lemon and olive couscous

Combine 1¼ cups couscous with 1¼ cups boiling water and 1 tablespoon oil in a large heatproof bowl, cover; stand about 5 minutes or until water is absorbed, fluffing with fork occasionally. Stir 400g (12½ ounces) rinsed, drained canned chickpeas (garbanzo beans), ½ cup coarsely chopped seeded green olives, 2 tablespoons lemon juice, 3 thinly sliced green onions (scallions), 2 tablespoons finely chopped fresh flat-leaf parsley and 1 tablespoon thinly sliced preserved lemon rind into the couscous. Season to taste.

prep time 15 minutes **serves** 6
nutritional count per serving 5.4g total fat (0.8g saturated fat); 1113kJ (266 cal); 41.8g carbohydrate; 9.8g protein; 6.1g fibre

spicy red couscous

Heat 1 tablespoon olive oil in a medium saucepan, add 2 teaspoons harissa paste, 2 teaspoons sweet paprika and 2 thinly sliced green onions (scallions); cook, stirring, about 2 minutes or until fragrant. Add 1 cup chicken stock and ½ cup water; bring to the boil. Remove from heat, add 1½ cups couscous; cover, stand about 5 minutes or until liquid is absorbed, fluffing with fork occasionally. Stir 1 tablespoon lemon juice into couscous; season to taste. Serve sprinkled with 2 finely sliced green onions.

prep + cook time 15 minutes **serves** 6
nutritional count per serving 3.7g total fat (0.6g saturated fat); 900kJ (215 cal); 37.4g carbohydrate; 6.2g protein; 2.6g fibre

tip Harissa is a hot paste; there are many different brands available on the market, and the strengths vary enormously. If you have a low heat-level tolerance, you may find this, and any other recipe containing harissa, too hot to tolerate, even if you reduce the amount.

pine nut and dried fig couscous

Bring 1 cup chicken stock to the boil in a medium saucepan. Remove from heat, add 1 cup couscous, cover; stand about 5 minutes or until liquid is absorbed, fluffing with fork occasionally. Stir ⅔ cup coarsely chopped dried figs, ½ cup toasted pine nuts, 2 teaspoons finely grated lemon rind, ¼ cup lemon juice and ¼ cup finely chopped fresh flat-leaf parsley into couscous; season to taste.

prep + cook time 15 minutes **serves** 4
nutritional count per serving 9.9g total fat (0.7g saturated fat); 1179kJ (282 cal); 38.5g carbohydrate; 7.4g protein; 4.2g fibre

tip Add your favourite dried fruit or nuts to the couscous. Serve warm or cold.

sides

spicy roasted pumpkin couscous

1 tablespoon olive oil

1 large red onion (300g), sliced thickly

2 cloves garlic, crushed

500g (1 pound) pumpkin, chopped coarsely

3 teaspoons ground cumin

2 teaspoons ground coriander

1 cup (200g) couscous

1 cup (250ml) boiling water

20g (¾ ounce) butter

2 tablespoons finely chopped fresh flat-leaf parsley

1 Preheat oven to 220°C/400°F.
2 Heat oil in a medium flameproof baking dish; cook onion, garlic and pumpkin, stirring, until vegetables are browned lightly. Add spices; cook, stirring, about 2 minutes or until fragrant. Transfer to oven; roast pumpkin mixture, uncovered, about 15 minutes or until pumpkin is just tender.
3 Meanwhile, combine couscous with the boiling water and butter in a large heatproof bowl; cover, stand about 5 minutes or until water is absorbed, fluffing with fork occasionally.
4 Stir pumpkin mixture and parsley into couscous.

prep + cook time 30 minutes **serves** 4
nutritional count per serving 9.5g total fat (3.7g saturated fat); 1342kJ (321 cal); 47.8g carbohydrate; 9.4g protein; 2.7g fibre

sides

READY IN
30
MINUTES

couscous salad with mixed peas and beans

Combine 1 cup couscous, 2 tablespoons lemon juice and 1 cup boiling water in a medium heatproof bowl; stand about 5 minutes or until liquid is absorbed, fluffing with fork occasionally, cool. Boil, steam or microwave 150g (4½ ounces) trimmed, halved baby beans and 150g (4½ ounces) trimmed sugar snap peas, separately, until just tender; drain. Rinse under cold water; drain. Combine 1½ tablespoons wholegrain mustard and ¼ cup olive oil in a large bowl; add couscous, beans, peas and ¼ cup finely chopped fresh chives, toss gently to combine.

prep + cook time 25 minutes (+ cooling) **serves** 8
nutritional count per serving 7.2g total fat (1g saturated fat); 748kJ (179 cal); 22g carbohydrate; 5.2g protein; 2.2g fibre

pilaf

Melt 20g (¾ ounce) butter in a medium saucepan; cook 1 clove crushed garlic, stirring, until fragrant. Add 1 cup basmati rice; cook, stirring, 1 minute. Add 1 cup chicken stock and 1 cup water; bring to the boil. Reduce heat; simmer, covered, about 20 minutes or until rice is just tender. Remove from heat; fluff rice with fork. Stir in ¼ cup coarsely chopped fresh flat-leaf parsley and ¼ cup toasted flaked almonds.

prep + cook time 30 minutes **serves** 4
nutritional count per serving 8.1g total fat (3g saturated fat); 1092kJ (261 cal); 41.2g carbohydrate; 5g protein; 1.5g fibre

rice and peas

Combine 1½ cups water, 1½ cups chicken stock and ¼ cup olive oil in a medium saucepan; bring to the boil. Stir in 2 cups white medium-grain rice; cook, uncovered, without stirring, about 10 minutes or until liquid has almost evaporated. Reduce heat; simmer, covered, 5 minutes. Meanwhile, trim and chop 4 green onions (scallions). Gently stir in onion and 1 cup frozen peas; simmer, covered, about 5 minutes or until rice and peas are tender. Season to taste.

prep + cook time 30 minutes **serves** 6
nutritional count per serving 9.8g total fat (1.6g saturated fat); 1437kJ (343 cal); 56.1g carbohydrate; 6.1g protein; 2.5g fibre

yellow coconut rice

Stand 1¾ cups white long-grain rice in a large bowl of cold water 30 minutes. Rinse rice under cold water until water runs clear; drain. Place 1¼ cups water, 1⅔ cups coconut cream, 1 teaspoon each white sugar and salt, ½ teaspoon ground turmeric, a pinch saffron threads and rice in a large heavy-based saucepan; cover, bring to the boil, stirring occasionally. Reduce heat; simmer, covered, without stirring, about 15 minutes or until rice is tender. Remove from heat; stand, covered, 5 minutes. Season to taste.

prep + cook time 20 minutes (+ standing) **serves** 4
nutritional count per serving 20.2g total fat (17.8g saturated fat); 1999kJ (477 cal); 66.9g carbohydrate; 6.5g protein; 1.4g fibre

sides

steamed ginger rice

Heat 1 tablespoon olive oil in a medium saucepan; cook 6 thinly sliced green onions (scallions), stirring, until softened. Add 2½ teaspoons finely grated fresh ginger and 1½ cups basmati rice; stir to coat in oil. Add 2 cups chicken stock; bring to the boil. Reduce heat; simmer, covered, over low heat, 10 minutes. Remove from heat; stand, covered, 5 minutes, then fluff with fork; stir in 2 tablespoons each finely chopped fresh coriander (cilantro) and mint, season to taste.

prep + cook time 20 minutes **serves** 4
nutritional count per serving 5.5g total fat (0.9g saturated fat); 1342kJ (321 cal); 61g carbohydrate; 5.7g protein; 1.1g fibre

pea mash

Place 1kg (2 pounds) coarsely chopped peeled pontiac potatoes in a medium saucepan with enough cold water to barely cover potato. Boil, uncovered, over medium heat, about 15 minutes or until potato is almost tender. Add 1½ cups frozen peas to potato; boil, uncovered, 3 minutes or until tender; drain. Mash potato mixture with 50g (1½ ounces) butter and ¾ cup hot milk; stir in peas.

prep + cook time 30 minutes **serves** 4
nutritional count per serving 12.4g total fat (7.9g saturated fat); 1183kJ (283 cal); 31.1g carbohydrate; 9g protein; 5.8g fibre

tip Any all-round or mashing potato is fine to use here. Desiree or sebago are also good choices.

celeriac mash

Place 800g (1½ pounds) coarsely chopped peeled potatoes in a medium saucepan with enough cold water to barely cover potatoes. Boil, uncovered, over medium heat about 15 minutes or until potato is tender. Drain. Meanwhile, boil, steam or microwave 1kg (2 pounds) coarsely chopped peeled celeriac until tender; drain. Mash potato and celeriac in a large bowl; stir in 60g (2 ounces) butter and ½ cup hot pouring cream. Drizzle with 2 teaspoons olive oil, and sprinkle with cracked black pepper to taste.

prep + cook time 30 minutes **serves** 6
nutritional count per serving 17.6g total fat (8.6g saturated fat); 1226kJ (293 cal); 23.5g carbohydrate; 5.7g protein; 9g fibre

spinach mash

Place 1kg (2 pounds) coarsely chopped peeled pontiac potatoes in a medium saucepan with enough cold water to barely cover potato. Boil, uncovered, over medium heat about 15 minutes or until potato is tender; drain. Meanwhile, boil, steam or microwave 200g (6½ ounces) baby spinach leaves until wilted; drain. Squeeze out excess liquid. Blend or process spinach with 40g (1½ ounces) butter until almost smooth. Mash potato in a large bowl; stir in ¼ teaspoon nutmeg and ½ cup hot pouring cream and spinach mixture. Season to taste.

prep + cook time 30 minutes **serves** 4
nutritional count per serving 22.1g total fat (14.3g saturated fat); 1430kJ (342 cal); 27.5g carbohydrate; 6.7g protein; 4.6g fibre

tip Any all-round or mashing potato is fine to use here. Desiree or sebago are also good choices.

potato puree

Place 1kg (2 pounds) coarsely chopped peeled potatoes in a medium saucepan with enough cold water to barely cover the potato. Boil, uncovered, over medium heat, about 15 minutes or until potato is tender; drain. Using the back of a wooden spoon, push potato through a fine sieve into a large bowl. Stir 40g (1½ ounces) butter and ¾ cup hot milk into potato, folding gently until mash is smooth and fluffy.

prep + cook time 30 minutes **serves** 4
nutritional count per serving 10.2g total fat (6.6g saturated fat); 991kJ (237 cal); 28.4g carbohydrate; 6.4g protein; 3.2g fibre

tip We used lasoda potatoes, but use any general purpose or mashing variety – desiree, sebago, coliban and king edward are all fine to use.

parsnip mash

Boil, steam or microwave 1kg (2 pounds) coarsely chopped peeled parsnips until tender; drain. Mash parsnip with 40g (1½ ounces) butter, 1 crushed garlic clove and ¾ cup hot pouring cream. To serve, sprinkle with 1 tablespoon torn parsley leaves, and cracked black pepper to taste.

prep + cook time 30 minutes **serves** 4
nutritional count per serving 10.5g total fat (6.6g saturated fat); 955kJ (228 cal); 24.9g carbohydrate; 5.7g protein; 5.9g fibre

fetta and black olive mash

Boil, steam or microwave 1kg (2 pounds) coarsely chopped peeled potatoes until tender; drain. Mash potato in a large bowl with 1 tablespoon olive oil until smooth. Stir in ⅔ cup warmed buttermilk, 200g (6½ ounces) finely chopped fetta cheese and ½ cup thinly sliced black olives. Drizzle with another tablespoon of olive oil. Season to taste.

prep + cook time 30 minutes **serves** 4
nutritional count per serving 25.5g total fat (10g saturated fat); 1865kJ (446 cal); 33.7g carbohydrate; 16.6g protein; 4.8g fibre

wasabi mash

Boil, steam or microwave 1kg (2 pounds) coarsely chopped peeled desiree potatoes until tender; drain. Place hot potato in a large bowl; mash until smooth, stir in ⅔ cup warm pouring cream and 1½ teaspoons wasabi paste. Season to taste.

prep + cook time 30 minutes **serves** 4
nutritional count per serving 14.7g total fat (9.2g saturated fat); 1255kJ (300 cal); 32.5g carbohydrate; 6.7g protein; 4.2g fibre

tip Any all-round or mashing potato is fine to use here. Pontiac or sebago are also good choices.

pumpkin mash

Boil, steam or microwave 500g (1 pound) coarsely chopped peeled pontiac potatoes and 500g (1 pound) coarsely chopped peeled pumpkin together until tender; drain. Mash potato and pumpkin; stir in 30g (1 ounce) butter. Season to taste.

prep + cook time 30 minutes **serves** 4
nutritional count per serving 6.5g total fat (2.6g saturated fat); 800kJ (191 cal); 25.6g carbohydrate; 4.7g protein; 5.3g fibre

tip Any all-round or mashing potato is fine to use here. Desiree or sebago are also good choices.

kumara mash

Boil, steam or microwave 500g (1 pound) coarsely chopped peeled kumara and 500g (1 pound) coarsely chopped peeled potatoes together until tender; drain. Mash in a large heatproof bowl. Combine ¼ cup chicken stock and 40g (1½ ounces) butter in a small saucepan over medium high heat until butter is melted. Stir into kumara mixture until combined. Season to taste.

prep + cook time 30 minutes **serves** 4
nutritional count per serving 8.5g total fat (5.4g saturated fat); 1024kJ (245 cal); 34.2g carbohydrate; 5.6g protein; 4.3g fibre

roasted capsicum mash

Quarter 2 medium red capsicums; discard seeds and membranes. Roast under hot grill, skin-side up, until skin blisters and blackens. Cover capsicum with plastic or paper for 5 minutes, then peel away skin. Blend capsicum until smooth. Meanwhile, boil, steam or microwave 1kg (2 pounds) coarsely chopped peeled potatoes until tender, drain. Mash potato; stir in ½ cup hot pouring cream and 20g (¾ ounce) softened butter. Add capsicum; stir until combined. Season to taste.

prep + cook time 30 minutes **serves** 4
nutritional count per serving 18g total fat (11.6g saturated fat); 1446kJ (346 cal); 36.2g carbohydrate; 7.7g protein; 4.7g fibre

fennel mash

Thinly slice 1 large fennel bulb; reserve 1 tablespoon fennel fronds. Melt 60g (2 ounces) butter in a large frying pan; cook fennel, covered, over low heat, about 10 minutes or until fennel is very soft. Blend or process fennel until smooth. Meanwhile, boil, steam or microwave 1kg (2 pounds) coarsely chopped peeled potatoes until tender; drain. Mash potato in a large heatproof bowl; stir in fennel mixture and ½ cup hot pouring cream. Season to taste; sprinkle with fennel fronds.

prep + cook time 30 minutes **serves** 4
nutritional count per serving 13.8g total fat (8.9g saturated fat); 1296kJ (310 cal); 36g carbohydrate; 7.3g protein; 6.1g fibre

white bean puree

Melt 20g (¾ ounce) butter in a medium frying pan; cook 1 finely chopped small brown onion and 1 crushed garlic clove, stirring, until onion softens. Add ¼ cup dry white wine; cook, stirring, until liquid is reduced by half. Add ¾ cup chicken stock and 800g (1½ pounds) rinsed and drained canned white beans; bring to the boil. Reduce heat; simmer, uncovered, about 10 minutes or until liquid is almost evaporated. Blend or process bean mixture and 2 tablespoons cream until smooth. Season to taste. Top with thinly sliced green onions (scallions) to serve.

prep + cook time 25 minutes **serves** 4
nutritional count per serving 7.1g total fat (3g saturated fat); 825kJ (197 cal); 18.6g carbohydrate; 10.6g protein; 9.8g fibre

spiced lentils

Cook 1½ cups red lentils, uncovered, in a large saucepan of boiling water until just tender; drain. Meanwhile, melt 25g (¾ ounce) butter in a large frying pan; cook 1 finely chopped small brown onion, 1 clove crushed garlic, ½ teaspoon each ground coriander and cumin, and ¼ teaspoon each ground turmeric and cayenne pepper, stirring, until onion softens. Add lentils, ½ cup chicken stock and an extra 25g (¾ ounce) butter; cook, stirring, until hot. Remove pan from heat, stir in 2 tablespoons coarsely chopped fresh flat-leaf parsley.

prep + cook time 20 minutes **serves** 4
nutritional count per serving 11.9g total fat (7g saturated fat); 1354kJ (324 cal); 29.9g carbohydrate; 18.9g protein; 10.8g fibre

peas with mint butter

Boil, steam or microwave 2¼ cups fresh shelled peas until tender; drain. Meanwhile, combine 40g (1½ ounces) butter, 1 tablespoon finely chopped fresh mint and 1 tablespoon thinly sliced lemon rind in a small bowl. Serve peas topped with butter mixture.

prep + cook time 10 minutes **serves** 4
nutritional count per serving 8.6g total fat (5.4g saturated fat); 589kJ (141 cal); 8.6g carbohydrate; 5.2g protein; 5g fibre

tip You need approximately 1kg (2 pounds) fresh pea pods to get the amount of shelled peas needed for this recipe.

brussels sprouts with cream and almonds

Melt 10g (½ ounce) butter in a large frying pan; cook ⅓ cup flaked almonds, stirring, until browned lightly; remove from pan. Melt 40g (1½ ounce) extra butter in same pan; cook 1kg (2 pounds) halved brussels sprouts and 2 crushed garlic cloves, stirring, until sprouts are browned lightly. Add 300ml (½ pint) pouring cream; bring to the boil. Reduce heat; simmer, uncovered, until sprouts are tender and sauce thickens slightly. Serve sprout mixture sprinkled with nuts.

prep + cook time 10 minutes **serves** 4
nutritional count per serving 46.7g total fat (28.4g saturated fat); 2061kJ (493 cal); 6.6g carbohydrate; 9.5g protein; 7.3g fibre

cauliflower gratin

Preheat oven to 220°C/400°F. Boil, steam or microwave 6 trimmed baby cauliflowers until tender; drain. Place in a medium shallow ovenproof dish. Meanwhile, melt 50g (1½ ounces) butter in a medium saucepan, add ¼ cup plain (all-purpose) flour; cook, stirring, until mixture bubbles and thickens. Gradually stir in 1¾ cups hot milk until smooth; cook, stirring, until mixture boils and thickens. Remove from heat; stir in ½ cup coarsely grated cheddar cheese and ¼ cup finely grated parmesan cheese. Pour cheese sauce over cauliflower in dish; sprinkle with 1 tablespoon japanese (panko) breadcrumbs. Bake about 15 minutes or until browned lightly.

prep + cook time 30 minutes **serves** 6
nutritional count per serving 18g total fat (10.1g saturated fat); 1121kJ (268 cal); 12.4g carbohydrate; 12.7g protein; 3.7g fibre

tip If you are unable to buy baby cauliflower, cut 750g (1½ pounds) cauliflower into florets.

fried cauliflower

To make batter, whisk 2 eggs, ½ cup self-raising flour and ½ cup water in a medium shallow bowl until smooth. Stir in 2 tablespoons finely chopped fresh coriander (cilantro); season. Heat enough vegetable oil to come half way up a wok. Dip 900g (1¾ pounds) cauliflower florets in batter; drain off excess. Deep-fry cauliflower, in batches, until browned lightly and tender. Drain on absorbent paper. Combine 2 tablespoons very finely chopped coriander (cilantro) and 1 cup greek-style yogurt in a small bowl; season to taste. Serve cauliflower with coriander yogurt.

prep + cook time 15 minutes **serves** 4
nutritional count per serving 9g total fat (2.8g saturated fat); 1083kJ (259 cal); 27.4g carbohydrate; 14.2g protein; 5.2g fibre

creamed spinach

Melt 20g (¾ ounce) butter in a large frying pan; cook 600g (1¼ pounds) trimmed spinach, stirring, until wilted. Add ½ cup pouring cream; bring to the boil. Reduce heat; simmer, uncovered, until liquid reduces by half.

prep + cook time 15 minutes **serves** 4
nutritional count per serving 38.7g total fat (25.4g saturated fat); 1555kJ (372 cal); 2.8g carbohydrate; 3.5g protein; 2.1g fibre

orange and maple-glazed baby carrots

Melt 30g (1 ounce) butter in a large frying pan over medium heat; cook 750g (1½ pounds) trimmed baby carrots, turning occasionally, about 8 minutes or until almost tender. Add 2 teaspoons finely grated orange rind, ¼ cup orange juice, 2 tablespoons dry white wine and 2 tablespoons maple syrup to pan; bring to the boil. Reduce heat; simmer, uncovered, until liquid has almost evaporated and carrots are tender and caramelised. Serve carrots sprinkled with ½ cup coarsely chopped roasted hazelnuts.

prep + cook time 25 minutes **serves** 4
nutritional count per serving 17.2g total fat (4.5g saturated fat); 1145kJ (274 cal); 20.8g carbohydrate; 4.1g protein; 7.7g fibre

asparagus hollandaise

To make hollandaise sauce, combine 2 tablespoons each of water, white wine vinegar and ¼ teaspoon cracked black pepper in a small saucepan; bring to the boil. Reduce heat; simmer, uncovered, until liquid is reduced to 1 tablespoon. Strain mixture through a fine sieve into a medium heatproof bowl; cool 10 minutes. Whisk 2 egg yolks into vinegar mixture. Set bowl over medium saucepan of simmering water (don't let water touch base of bowl). Whisk mixture over heat until thickened. Remove bowl from heat; gradually whisk in 200g (6½ ounces) melted butter in a thin, steady stream, whisking constantly until sauce is thick and creamy. Boil, steam or microwave 1kg (2 pounds) trimmed asparagus until tender. Serve asparagus on a large platter drizzled with hollandaise sauce; season to taste with cracked black pepper.

prep + cook time 35 minutes **serves** 4
nutritional count per serving 44g total fat (26.9g saturated fat); 1797kJ (430 cal); 2.8g carbohydrate; 6.1g protein; 2.6g fibre

prosciutto-wrapped bean bundles

Cook 200g (6½ ounces) each of trimmed green and yellow beans in a medium saucepan of boiling water until just tender; drain. Rinse under cold water; drain. Divide beans into eight equal bundles. Place 8 prosciutto slices on a board; top each with one bean bundle. Wrap beans with prosciutto, rolling to enclose beans tightly. Cook bean bundles in a heated oiled large frying pan, over high heat, turning, until prosciutto is crisp. Remove from pan; cover to keep warm. Melt 60g (2 ounces) butter in the same pan; cook 1 tablespoon rinsed, drained baby capers, stirring, 1 minute. Stir in 1 tablespoon lemon juice. Serve bean bundles drizzled with caper mixture; sprinkle with ⅓ cup coarsely chopped fresh flat-leaf parsley.

prep + cook time 30 minutes **serves** 8
nutritional count per serving 6.9g total fat (4.3g saturated fat); 347kJ (83 cal); 1.5g carbohydrate; 3.3g protein; 1.5g fibre

garlicky beans with pine nuts

Boil, steam or microwave 400g (12½ ounces) trimmed baby beans until just tender; drain. Add beans to a large bowl of iced water; drain well. Place in a large bowl. Heat ¼ cup olive oil and 1 thinly sliced clove garlic in a small frying pan over low heat until garlic just changes colour. Add 2 tablespoons roasted pine nuts; stir until heated through. Drizzle mixture over beans.

prep + cook time 20 minutes **serves** 4
nutritional count per serving 18.9g total fat (2.2g saturated fat); 828kJ (198 cal); 2.8g carbohydrate; 3.2g protein; 3.2g fibre

mixed bean salad with hazelnut butter

Boil, steam or microwave 250g (8 ounces) each of trimmed green beans and yellow beans until tender; drain. Combine warm beans with 60g (2 ounces) chopped butter, ⅓ cup finely chopped roasted hazelnuts, ½ cup torn flat-leaf parsley and 2 teaspoons finely grated lemon rind in a medium bowl.

prep + cook time 15 minutes **serves** 4
nutritional count per serving 19.5g total fat (8.4g saturated fat); 907kJ (217 cal); 3.8g carbohydrate; 4.7g protein; 5g fibre

lime and coconut snake bean salad

Boil, steam or microwave 350g (11 ounces) coarsely chopped snake beans until tender; drain. Meanwhile, combine ¼ cup coconut cream, 1 tablespoon lime juice, 2 teaspoons fish sauce and 1 thinly sliced long red chilli in a screw-top jar; shake well. Combine beans, coconut mixture, ½ cup coarsely shredded fresh coconut and ¾ cup loosely packed fresh coriander leaves (cilantro) in a medium bowl.

prep + cook time 20 minutes **serves** 4
nutritional count per serving 11.5g total fat (9.9g saturated fat); 598kJ (143 cal); 3.2g carbohydrate; 4.5g protein; 4.9g fibre

tip To open a fresh coconut, pierce one of the eyes then roast coconut briefly in a very hot oven only until cracks appear in the shell. Cool the coconut, then break it apart and grate the flesh.

steamed gai lan in oyster sauce

Boil, steam or microwave 1kg (2 pounds) halved gai lan until tender; drain. Heat 1 tablespoon peanut oil in a wok; stir-fry gai lan, 2 tablespoons oyster sauce and 1 tablespoon light soy sauce about 2 minutes or until mixture is heated through.

prep + cook time 10 minutes **serves** 8
nutritional count per serving 2.6g total fat (0.4g saturated fat); 205kJ (49 cal); 2.7g carbohydrate; 2.3g protein; 2.4g fibre

steamed asian greens with char siu sauce

Layer 350g (11 ounces) trimmed broccolini, 150g (5 ounces) trimmed snow peas, 2 halved baby buk choy and 1 thinly sliced fresh long red chilli in a large baking-paper-lined bamboo steamer. Steam, covered, over a large wok of simmering water about 5 minutes or until vegetables are just tender. Combine vegetables, 2 tablespoons char siu sauce and 2 teaspoons sesame oil in a large bowl. Heat 1 tablespoon peanut oil in a small saucepan until hot; pour oil over vegetable mixture then toss to combine. Serve sprinkled with 1 tablespoon toasted sesame seeds.

prep + cook time 25 minutes **serves** 4
nutritional count per serving 9.5g total fat (1.4g saturated fat); 635kJ (152 cal); 7g carbohydrate; 6.6g protein; 6.6g fibre

grilled asian vegetables

Boil, steam or microwave 400g (12½ ounces) trimmed, halved baby pak choy until wilted; drain. Brush with 1 tablespoon peanut oil; cook on a heated oiled flat plate until tender. Cut 200g (6½ ounces) baby corn in half lengthways; combine in a large bowl with 175g (5½ ounces) halved broccolini, 100g (3 ounces) trimmed snow peas and an extra 1 tablespoon peanut oil; mix well. Cook vegetables on a flat plate until tender. Meanwhile, combine 2 tablespoons mirin, 1 tablespoon each of oyster sauce and light soy sauce, 1 clove crushed garlic, 1 teaspoon white sugar and ½ teaspoon sesame oil in same bowl; mix in vegetables.

prep + cook time 25 minutes **serves** 4
nutritional count per serving 11.2g total fat (1.9g saturated fat); 948kJ (226 cal); 16.7g carbohydrate; 8.7g protein; 8.6g fibre

tips Rösti are best made from a starchy potato, such as coliban, sebago, russet burbank or desiree. Do not grate the potato until ready to cook to avoid discolouring. Perfect rösti have a thick crunchy crust and are moist and buttery inside. While best served immediately, they can be kept, loosely covered with foil, in a slow oven for up to an hour.

the perfect rösti

1kg (2 pounds) potatoes

1 teaspoon salt

80g (2½ ounces) unsalted butter

2 tablespoons vegetable oil

1 Grate potatoes coarsely into a large bowl, stir in salt; squeeze excess moisture from potatoes. Divide potato mixture into eight portions.
2 Heat 10g (½ ounce) of the butter and 1 teaspoon of the oil in a medium frying pan; spread one portion of the potato mixture over base of pan, flatten with a spatula or egg slice to form a firm pancake.
3 Cook, uncovered, over medium heat, until golden brown on the underside; shake pan to loosen rösti, then invert onto a large plate. Gently slide rösti back into pan; cook, uncovered, until other side is golden brown and potato centre is tender. Drain on absorbent paper; cover to keep warm.
4 Repeat to make a total of eight rösti.

prep + cook time 25 minutes **makes** 8
nutritional count per rösti 13g total fat (6.1g saturated fat); 828kJ (198 cal); 16.4g carbohydrate; 3.1g protein; 2g fibre

READY IN 30 MINUTES

potato salad with herbed cream

To make herbed cream, combine ½ cup each of mayonnaise and sour cream, ¼ cup warm water, 3 teaspoons dijon mustard, ¼ cup finely chopped fresh chives and ½ cup coarsely chopped fresh flat-leaf parsley in a screw-top jar; shake well. Boil, steam or microwave 1.5kg (3 pounds) scrubbed, unpeeled medium kipfler potatoes until tender; drain. Cool, then slice potatoes crossways into 2cm (¾-inch) thick rounds. Drizzle potato with herbed cream.

prep + cook time 25 minutes **serves** 8
nutritional count per serving 12.2g total fat (4.6g saturated fat); 1074kJ (257 cal); 29g carbohydrate; 5.2g protein; 4.1g fibre

sautéed potatoes

Cut 1kg (2 pounds) unpeeled desiree potatoes into 1cm (½-inch) slices. Heat 2 tablespoons olive oil and 50g (1½ ounces) chopped butter in a large frying pan; cook potato, covered, over medium-low heat, turning occasionally, about 10 minutes or until browned lightly and tender.

prep + cook time 25 minutes **serves** 4
nutritional count per serving 19.6g total fat (5.9g saturated fat); 1395kJ (333 cal); 30.9g carbohydrate; 5.8g protein; 4.2g fibre

tip Sautéed potatoes are quick and easy to make. You can also use ghee, unsalted butter or a mixture of butter and oil, if you prefer, because all can be used over high heat without burning. You can also use sebago potatoes for this recipe.

lyonnaise potatoes

Boil, steam or microwave 900g (1¾ pounds) coarsely chopped peeled desiree potatoes until just tender; drain. Meanwhile, heat 2 teaspoons olive oil in a large frying pan; cook 2 thinly sliced medium red onions and 3 cloves crushed garlic, stirring, until onion softens. Remove from pan. Cook 6 coarsely chopped rindless bacon slices in the same pan, stirring, until crisp; drain on absorbent paper. Heat an extra 2 teaspoons olive oil in the same pan; cook potato, stirring, about 5 minutes or until browned lightly. Return onion mixture and bacon to pan; stir gently to combine with potato. Remove from heat; stir in ¼ cup coarsely chopped fresh mint.

prep + cook time 30 minutes **serves** 4
nutritional count per serving 18.8g total fat (6g saturated fat); 1754kJ (419 cal); 32g carbohydrate; 26.9g protein; 5.9g fibre

tip You can also use sebage or ruby lou potatoes.

tomato and herb salad

Place 5 coarsely chopped medium tomatoes, 2 tablespoons coarsely chopped fresh mint, ¼ cup coarsely chopped fresh flat-leaf parsley and 2 tablespoons finely chopped fresh dill in a medium bowl. Place 2 cloves crushed garlic, 2 tablespoons lemon juice, 1 tablespoon olive oil and 2 teaspoons white vinegar in a screw-top jar; shake well. Drizzle dressing over salad; toss gently to combine.

prep time 10 minutes **serves** 4
nutritional count per serving 4.9g total fat (0.7g saturated fat); 362kJ (87 cal); 5.7g carbohydrate; 2.6g protein; 3.5g fibre

bean and tomato salad with hazelnut dressing

Combine ½ cup roasted, skinned, coarsely chopped hazelnuts, 2 tablespoons each of hazelnut oil and apple cider vinegar and 1 teaspoon wholegrain mustard in a screw-top jar; shake well. Boil, steam or microwave 200g (6½ ounces) trimmed green beans until tender; drain. Rinse under cold water; drain. Combine beans, 250g (8 ounces) quartered cherry tomatoes and hazelnut mixture in a medium bowl; toss gently to combine.

prep + cook time 20 minutes **serves** 4
nutritional count per serving 20.2g total fat (1.8g saturated fat); 920kJ (220 cal); 3.6g carbohydrate; 4.2g protein; 4.3g fibre

oak leaf and mixed herb salad with dijon vinaigrette

Combine 2 tablespoons each of olive oil and white wine vinegar with 1 tablespoon dijon mustard and 2 teaspoons white (granulated) sugar in a screw-top jar; shake well. Combine dijon mixture with 1 green oak leaf lettuce, leaves separated, ¼ cup coarsely chopped fresh chives, ½ cup each of firmly packed fresh flat-leaf parsley and fresh chervil leaves in a medium bowl; toss gently to combine.

prep time 10 minutes **serves** 6
nutritional count per serving 6.2g total fat (0.9g saturated fat); 288kJ (69 cal); 2g carbohydrate; 0.7g protein; 1.1g fibre

baby spinach and parmesan salad

Place 100g (3 ounces) baby spinach leaves, 50g (1½ ounces) shaved parmesan cheese and 1 tablespoon toasted pine nuts in a large bowl. Combine 2 tablespoons balsamic vinegar and 1 tablespoon olive oil in a screw-top jar; shake well, season to taste. Drizzle dressing over salad; toss gently to combine.

prep time 10 minutes **serves** 4
nutritional count per serving 13.4g total fat (1.3g saturated fat); 561kJ (134 cal); 0.7g carbohydrate; 2.3g protein; 1.1g fibre

coleslaw

Place 2 tablespoons mayonnaise and 1 tablespoon white wine vinegar in a screw-top jar; shake well. Place dressing in a large bowl with 2 cups finely shredded white cabbage, 1 cup finely shredded red cabbage, 1 coarsely grated medium carrot and 3 thinly sliced green onions (scallions); toss gently to combine.

prep time 15 minutes **serves** 4
nutritional count per serving 3.1g total fat (0.4g saturated fat); 251kJ (60 cal); 4.9g carbohydrate; 1.6g protein; 3.3g fibre

sides

glossary

artichoke hearts tender centre of the globe artichoke; purchased, in brine, canned or in glass jars.
bamboo shoots the tender shoots of bamboo plants, available in cans; must be rinsed and drained before use.
beans
butter also known as lima beans; large, flat, kidney-shaped bean, off-white in colour, with a mealy texture and mild taste.
cannellini a small white bean similar in appearance and flavour to other white beans (great northern, navy or haricot), all of which can be substituted for the other. Available dried or canned.
snake long (about 40cm/16 inches), thin, round, fresh green beans, Asian in origin, with a taste similar to green or french beans. Are also known as yard-long beans because of their (pre-metric) length.
sprouts also known as bean shoots; tender new growths of assorted beans and seeds germinated for consumption.
white see cannellini beans.
breadcrumbs
packaged fine-textured, crunchy, purchased white breadcrumbs.
panko also known as japanese breadcrumbs. They are available in two types: larger pieces and fine crumbs. Both have a lighter texture than Western-style breadcrumbs. They are at all Asian grocery stores and, unless you make rather coarse breadcrumbs from white bread that's either quite stale or gently toasted, nothing is an adequate substitute. Has a crunchy texture with a delicate, pale golden colour.
stale one- or two-day-old bread made into crumbs by blending or processing.
buk choy also known as bok choy, pak choi, chinese white cabbage or chinese chard; has a fresh, mild mustard taste. Use both stems and leaves. Baby buk choy, also known as pak kat farang or shanghai bok choy, is smaller and more tender than buk choy.
butter use salted or unsalted (sweet) butter; 125g is equal to one stick of butter (4 ounces).
cajun seasoning a blend of assorted herbs and spices that may include paprika, basil, onion, fennel, thyme, cayenne and tarragon.
caperberries the fruit formed after the caper buds have flowered; caperberries are pickled, usually with stalks intact.
capers grey-green buds of a warm climate shrub (usually Mediterranean); sold either dried and salted or pickled in a vinegar brine. Baby capers are very small and have a fuller flavour. Rinse well before using.
cheese
blue mould-treated cheeses mottled with blue veining. Varieties include firm and crumbly stilton types to mild, creamy brie-like cheeses.
cream cheese known as philadelphia or philly; a soft, cows'-milk cheese; sold at supermarkets. also available as a spreadable light cream cheese – a blend of cottage and cream cheeses.
fetta, danish (also danish white fetta) this type of fetta is a smooth and creamy variation of the more traditional fetta cheeses. The cheese is popular for its ability to be cubed and sliced without crumbling, and tossed into salads. Danish fetta has a very different taste to traditional fetta cheese. It has a milder taste, which makes it popular as an ingredient in baking.

fetta, persian a soft, creamy fetta marinated in a blend of olive oil, garlic, herbs and spices. It is available from most larger supermarkets.
goat's made from goat's milk, has an earthy, strong taste; available in both soft and firm textures, in various shapes and sizes, and sometimes rolled in ash or herbs.
gorgonzola a creamy blue cheese having a mild, sweet taste.
gruyère a Swiss cheese with small holes and a nutty, slightly salty flavour.
haloumi a firm, cream-coloured sheep-milk cheese matured in brine; haloumi can be grilled or fried, briefly, without breaking down. Should be eaten while still warm as it becomes tough and rubbery on cooling.
mascarpone a cultured cream product made in much the same way as yogurt. Is whitish to creamy yellow in colour, with a soft, creamy texture and a rich, sweet, slightly acidic, taste.
pizza a blend of grated mozzarella, cheddar and parmesan cheeses.
chilli generally, the smaller the chilli, the hotter it is. Use rubber gloves when seeding and chopping fresh chillies as they can burn your skin. Removing seeds and membranes lessens the heat level.
cayenne pepper a long, thin-fleshed, extremely hot red chilli usually sold dried and ground.
long available both fresh and dried; a generic term used for any moderately hot, long (6cm-8cm), thin chilli.
red thai a small, hot, bright red coloured chilli.
chinese barbecued pork also called char siew. Has a sweet-sticky coating made from soy sauce, sherry, five-spice powder and hoisin sauce. Available from Asian food stores.
chinese cooking wine also known as shao hsing or chinese rice wine; made from fermented rice, wheat, sugar and salt with a 13.5 per cent alcohol content. Inexpensive and found in Asian food shops; if you can't find it, replace with mirin or sherry.
chorizo a sausage of Spanish origin; made of coarsely ground pork and highly seasoned with garlic and chilli. They are deeply smoked, very spicy, and are available dry-cured or raw (which needs cooking).
coriander also known as pak chee, cilantro or chinese parsley; a bright-green leafy herb with a pungent flavour. Both the stems and roots of coriander are also used in cooking; wash well before using. Also available ground or as seeds; these should not be substituted for fresh coriander as the tastes are completely different.
cos lettuce also known as romaine.
couscous a fine, grain-like cereal product made from semolina.
cream we use fresh cream, also known as pure cream and pouring cream, unless otherwise stated.
cumin also known as zeera or comino; has a spicy, nutty flavour.
curry
curry powder a blend of ground spices used for convenience. Choose mild or hot to suit your taste.
green paste the hottest of the traditional pastes; contains chilli, garlic, onion, salt, lemon grass, spices and galangal.
tandoori paste a highly-seasoned classic East-Indian marinade flavoured with garlic, tamarind, ginger, coriander, chilli and other spices, and used to give foods the authentic red-orange tint of tandoor oven cooking.

tikka paste a medium-mild paste of chilli, coriander, cumin, lentil flour, garlic, ginger, turmeric, fennel, cloves, cinnamon and cardamom.
tom yum paste a Thai-style paste with a hot, spicy and sour flavour. Containing lemon grass, red chilli, sugar, onion, anchovy, galangal, kaffir lime and paprika. It is used to make the tradition spicy sour prawn soup known as tom yum goong.
eggplant also known as aubergine.
fennel also known as finocchio or anise; a white to very pale green-white, firm, crisp, roundish vegetable about 8-12cm in diameter. The bulb has a slightly sweet, anise flavour but the leaves have a much stronger taste. Also the name given to dried seeds having a licorice flavour.
fish fillets, firm white blue eye, bream, flathead, swordfish, ling, whiting, jewfish, snapper or sea perch are all good choices. Check for small pieces of bone and use tweezers to remove them.
five-spice powder also known as chinese five-spice; a fragrant mixture of ground cinnamon, cloves, star anise, sichuan pepper and fennel seeds.
flour
plain an all-purpose wheat flour.
self-raising plain flour sifted with baking powder in the proportion of 1 cup flour to 2 teaspoons baking powder.
ginger the thick root of a tropical plant; also known as root ginger.
gnocchi Italian 'dumplings' made of potatoes, semolina or flour.
kaffir lime leaves also known as bai magrood. Aromatic leaves of a citrus tree; two glossy dark green leaves joined end to end, forming a rounded hourglass shape. A strip of fresh lime peel may be substituted for each kaffir lime leaf.
kecap manis see sauces, soy.
kumara the Polynesian name of an orange-fleshed sweet potato often confused with yam.
lebanese cucumber short, slender and thin-skinned. Probably the most popular variety because of its tender, edible skin, tiny, yielding seeds and sweet, fresh flavoursome taste.
lemon grass a tall, clumping, lemon-smelling and -tasting, sharp-edged grass; the white lower part of the stem is used, finely chopped, in cooking.
lentils (red, brown, yellow) dried pulses often identified by and named after their colour; also known as dhal.
mayonnaise we use whole-egg mayonnaise in our recipes.
mesclun a salad mix or gourmet salad mix with a mixture of assorted young lettuce and other green leaves, including baby spinach leaves, mizuna and curly endive.
mince also known as ground meat.
mirin a Japanese champagne-coloured cooking wine; made of glutinous rice and alcohol and used expressly for cooking. Should not be confused with sake.
mushrooms
enoki clumps of long, spaghetti-like stems with tiny, snowy white caps.
flat large, flat mushrooms with a rich earthy flavour. They are sometimes misnamed field mushrooms, which are wild mushrooms.
oyster also known as abalone; grey-white mushroom shaped like a fan. Prized for their smooth texture and subtle, oyster-like flavour.
shiitake when fresh are also known as chinese black, forest or golden oak mushrooms; although cultivated, they are large and meaty and have the earthiness and taste of wild mushrooms. When dried, they are known as donko or dried chinese mushrooms; rehydrate before use.
swiss brown also known as cremini or roman mushrooms, are light brown mushrooms having a full-bodied flavour.
mustard seeds are available in black, brown or yellow varieties. They are available from major supermarkets and health-food shops.
noodles
bean thread vermicelli made from mung bean flour. Fine, delicate noodles also known as wun sen, cellophane or glass noodles (because they are transparent when cooked). available dried in various-sized bundles. Must be soaked to soften before use.
dried rice stick see rice vermicelli, dried (below).
egg, fresh also known as ba mee or yellow noodles. Made from wheat flour and eggs. Range in size from very fine strands to wide, thick spaghetti-like pieces as thick as a shoelace.
hokkien also known as stir-fry noodles; fresh wheat noodles resembling thick, yellow-brown spaghetti needing no pre-cooking.
ramen, fresh comes in various shapes and lengths. They may be fat, thin or even ribbon-like, as well as straight or wrinkled. While more often sold dried, fresh ramen is available from some Asian food stores. Substitute with reconstituted dried noodles.
rice vermicelli, dried very fine noodles made from rice flour and water, vermicelli are often compressed into tablets and dried. Before use they require soaking in boiling water until they are tender.
soba a thin spaghetti-like pale brown noodle from Japan; made from buckwheat and varying proportions of wheat flour.
onions
green also known as scallion or, incorrectly, shallot; an immature onion picked before the bulb has formed. Has a long, bright-green edible stalk.
red also known as spanish, red spanish or bermuda onion; a sweet-flavoured, large, purple-red onion.
shallots also called french shallots, golden shallots or eschalots; small, brown-skinned, elongated members of the onion family.
spring have small white bulbs and long, narrow, green-leafed tops.
pak choy similar to baby buk choy, except the stem is a very pale green, rather than white, and the top is less leafy.
paprika ground, dried, sweet red capsicum (bell pepper); there are many types available, including sweet, hot, mild and smoked.
parsley, flat-leaf also known as continental or italian parsley.
pasta
angel hair also known as barbina. Long, thin, delicate strands of spaghetti-like pasta.
fusilli also known as corkscrews. Dried spiral-shaped pasta.
orecchiette small disc-shaped pasta; translates literally as 'little ears'.
rigatoni a form of tube-shaped pasta. it is larger than penne and is usually ridged, the end doesn't terminate at an angle, like penne does.
peppercorns
pink dried berry from a type of rose plant grown in Madagascar, usually sold packed in brine; they possess a distinctive pungently sweet taste.

sichuan also known as chinese pepper. Small, red-brown aromatic seeds resembling black peppercorns; they have a peppery-lemon flavour.
pitta also known as lebanese bread.
pizza bases pre-packaged for home-made pizzas. They come in a variety of sizes (snack or family) and thicknesses (thin and crispy or thick).
polenta also known as cornmeal; a flour-like cereal made of ground corn (maize). Also the name of the dish made from it.
prawn also known as shrimp.
preserved lemon rind a North African specialty; lemons are quartered and preserved in salt and lemon juice or water. To use, remove and discard pulp, squeeze juice from rind, rinse rind well; slice thinly. Once opened, store under refrigeration.
prosciutto a kind of unsmoked italian ham; salted, air-cured and aged.
rice
basmati a white, fragrant long-grained rice. Wash several times before cooking.
jasmine fragrant long-grained rice; white rice can be substituted, but will not taste the same.
rocket also known as arugula, rugula and rucola; a peppery-tasting green leaf. Baby rocket leaves are both smaller and less peppery.
sake made from fermented rice. If sake is unavailable, dry sherry, vermouth or brandy can be substituted. Cooking sake (containing salt) is also available.
sambal oelek (also ulek or olek) Indonesian in origin; a salty paste made from ground chillies and vinegar. Found in supermarkets and Asian food stores.
sauces
black bean a Chinese sauce made from fermented soya beans, spices, water and wheat flour.
char siu a Chinese barbecue sauce made from sugar, water, salt, fermented soya bean paste, honey, soy sauce, malt syrup and spices. It can be found at most supermarkets.
fish also called nam pla or nuoc nam; made from pulverised salted fermented fish, most often anchovies. Has a pungent smell and strong taste, so use sparingly.
hoisin a thick, sweet and spicy Chinese paste made from salted fermented soya beans, onions and garlic.
oyster Asian in origin, this rich, brown sauce is made from oysters and their brine, cooked with salt and soy sauce, and thickened with starches.
plum a thick, sweet and sour dipping sauce made from plums, vinegar, sugar, chillies and spices.
soy made from fermented soya beans. Several variations are available in most supermarkets and Asian food stores. We use japanese soy sauce unless otherwise indicated. It is the best table soy and the one to choose if you only want one type.
dark soy deep brown, almost black in colour; rich, with a thicker consistency than other types. Pungent but not that salty.
japanese soy an all-purpose low-sodium soy sauce made with more wheat content than its Chinese counterparts.
kecap manis (ketjap manis); a thick soy sauce with added sugar and spices. The sweetness is derived from the addition of molasses or palm sugar.

light soy a fairly thin, pale but salty tasting sauce; used in dishes in which the natural colour of the ingredients is to be maintained. Do not confuse with salt-reduced or low-sodium soy sauces.
sweet chilli a mild sauce made from red chillies, sugar, garlic and vinegar.
silver beet also known as swiss chard; mistakenly called spinach.
snow peas also called mange tout (eat all). Snow pea tendrils, the growing shoots of the plant, are also available at greengrocers. Snow pea sprouts are the tender new growths of snow peas.
spinach also known as english spinach and, incorrectly, silver beet.
sugar
brown very soft, finely granulated sugar retaining molasses for its characteristic colour and flavour. Dark brown sugar may be substituted.
caster also known as superfine or finely granulated table sugar.
white a coarsely granulated table sugar, also known as crystal sugar.
sugar snap peas are also known as honey snap peas; fresh small peas that can be eaten whole, pod and all, similarly to snow peas.
sumac a purple-red, astringent spice ground from berries growing on shrubs that flourish wild around the mediterranean; adds a tart, lemony flavour to food. Available from spice shops and major supermarkets.
tahini a rich, sesame-seed paste, used in most Middle-Eastern cuisines, especially Lebanese, in dips and sauces.
turmeric related to galangal and ginger; adds a golden-yellow colour to food.
vinegar
balsamic originally from Modena, Italy, there are now many balsamic vinegars on the market ranging in pungency and quality depending on how long they have been aged. Is a deep rich brown colour and has a sweet and sour flavour. Quality can be determined up to a point by price; use the most expensive sparingly.
red wine based on fermented red wine.
rice a colourless vinegar made from fermented rice, sugar and salt. also known as seasoned rice vinegar.
white made from spirit of cane sugar.
white wine made from white wine.
vietnamese mint not a mint at all, but a pungent and peppery narrow-leafed member of the buckwheat family.
water chestnut resembles a chestnut in appearance, hence the English name. They are small brown tubers with a crisp, white, nutty-tasting flesh. Their crunchy texture is best experienced fresh, however, canned water chestnuts are more easily obtained and can be kept for about a month, once opened, under refrigeration.
white miso paste Japan's famous bean paste made from fermented soya beans and rice, rye or barley. It varies in colour, texture and saltiness. It is a common ingredient in soups, sauces and dressings. White miso tends to have a sweeter and somewhat less salty flavour than the darker red miso. Dissolve the miso in a little bit of water before adding. Keeps well refrigerated.
watercress one of the cress family, a large group of peppery greens. Highly perishable, so must be used as soon as possible after purchase.
wombok also known as peking cabbage, chinese cabbage or petsai. elongated in shape with pale green, crinkly leaves.

conversion chart

measures

One Australian metric measuring cup holds approximately 250ml; one Australian metric tablespoon holds 20ml; one Australian metric teaspoon holds 5ml. The difference between one country's measuring cups and another's is within a two- or three-teaspoon variance, and will not affect your cooking results. North America, New Zealand and the United Kingdom use a 15ml tablespoon.

All cup and spoon measurements are level. The most accurate way of measuring dry ingredients is to weigh them. When measuring liquids, use a clear glass or plastic jug with the metric markings.

The imperial measurements used in these recipes are approximate only. Measurements for cake pans are approximate only. Using same-shaped cake pans of a similar size should not affect the outcome of your baking. We measure the inside top of the cake pan to determine sizes.

We use large eggs with an average weight of 60g.

dry measures

metric	imperial
15g	½oz
30g	1oz
60g	2oz
90g	3oz
125g	4oz (¼lb)
155g	5oz
185g	6oz
220g	7oz
250g	8oz (½lb)
280g	9oz
315g	10oz
345g	11oz
375g	12oz (¾lb)
410g	13oz
440g	14oz
470g	15oz
500g	16oz (1lb)
750g	24oz (1½lb)
1kg	32oz (2lb)

liquid measures

metric	imperial
30ml	1 fluid oz
60ml	2 fluid oz
100ml	3 fluid oz
125ml	4 fluid oz
150ml	5 fluid oz
190ml	6 fluid oz
250ml	8 fluid oz
300ml	10 fluid oz
500ml	16 fluid oz
600ml	20 fluid oz
1000ml (1 litre)	1¾ pints

length measures

metric	imperial
3mm	⅛in
6mm	¼in
1cm	½in
2cm	¾in
2.5cm	1in
5cm	2in
6cm	2½in
8cm	3in
10cm	4in
13cm	5in
15cm	6in
18cm	7in
20cm	8in
22cm	9in
25cm	10in
28cm	11in
30cm	12in (1ft)

oven temperatures

The oven temperatures in this book are for conventional ovens; if you have a fan-forced oven, decrease the temperature by 10-20 degrees.

	°C (CELSIUS)	°F (FAHRENHEIT)
Very slow	120	250
Slow	150	300
Moderately slow	160	325
Moderate	180	350
Moderately hot	200	400
Hot	220	425
Very hot	240	475

index

A

asian greens
    grilled asian vegetables 227
    steamed asian greens with char siu sauce 227
    steamed gai lan in oyster sauce 226
    steamed orange ginger chicken with greens 16
asian mussels 151
asparagus hollandaise 224

B

bacon, leek and potato frittata 119
beans
    bean and basil soup 197
    couscous salad with mixed peas and beans 212
    garlicky beans with pine nuts 225
    green bean and tomato salad with hazelnut dressing 232
    lamb and black bean stir-fry with sambal 52
    lime and coconut snake bean salad 226
    mixed bean salad with hazelnut butter 225
    prosciutto-wrapped bean bundles 224
    white bean puree 220
beef
    beef and mixed sprout salad 78
    blue-cheese-stuffed beef with brandied figs 77
    creamy beef and mushroom rigatoni 89
    fajitas 95
    quesadillas 91
    quick beef pho 102
    sausage and crunchy slaw burgers 101
    sichuan beef stir-fry 86
    spicy beef kway teow 85
    steak and chips with a modern twist 74
    t-bone steaks with crispy shallots and horseradish mascarpone 81
    thai spicy beef and noodle stir-fry 99
    upside-down 92
    vietnamese beef salad 91
    warm roast beef and vegetable salad 96
blue cheese
    blue cheese and salami omelette 125
    blue cheese, apple and barbecued chicken slaw 33
    blue-cheese-stuffed beef with brandied figs 77
brussels sprouts
    cream and almonds with 221
    pork and brussels sprout stir-fry 126
burgers
    curry lemon chicken 30
    minty lamb 67
    sausage and crunchy slaw 101

C

cauliflower
    cauliflower and cheese pasta bake 181
    fried 222
    gratin 222
    pork chops with blue-cheese sauce and cauliflower mash 130
cheesy brioche toasts 193
cheesy pesto polenta 206
chicken
    blue cheese, apple and barbecued chicken slaw 33
    breasts with walnut pesto 22
    chermoulla barbecued chicken thighs 22
    chicken and potato salad 38
    chicken, fetta and mushroom pasta 33
    chicken satay skewers with crunchy salad 12
    chilli chicken san choy bow 29
    crisp parmesan chicken with eggplant salad 14
    curry lemon chicken burgers 30
    hoisin and lemon chicken skewers 41
    indian chicken pilaf 41
    jerk chicken with pumpkin and onion 14
    moroccan 42
    moroccan-spiced chicken casserole 26
    peri peri coconut chicken curry 37
    spanish chicken and chorizo stew 25
    steamed orange ginger chicken with greens 16
    thai chicken, papaya and peanut salad 19
    thighs with burnt-orange sauce 26
    vietnamese chicken and mango salad 10
chorizo
    chorizo, tomato and rocket pasta salad 137
    smoky prawn and chorizo stew 155
    spanish chicken and chorizo stew 25
coleslaw 233
couscous
    couscous salad with mixed peas and beans 212
    green onion 207
    lemon pistachio 208
    moroccan lamb cutlets with roasted capsicum couscous salad 51
    pine nut and dried fig 209
    preserved lemon and olive 208
    spicy red 209
    spicy roasted pumpkin couscous 210
crêpes, curried pumpkin 199
curried pumpkin crêpes 199
curried vegetable and lentil soup 190
curry
    curry lemon chicken burgers 30
    korma curry meatballs 52
    korma prawn 166
    paneer and vegetable curry 189
    peri peri coconut chicken curry 37
    pork and mango 125

D

dressing
    chilli 156
    chilli lime 12
    green pesto 48
    lemon 59, 82, 147
    mustard horseradish 96
    soy lime 78
    soy sesame 16
    tzatziki 47
duck breasts with roasted vegetables 19

E

eggplant, spicy, with soft-boiled eggs and labne 200
eggs, see also frittata
    blue cheese and salami omelette 125
    spicy eggplant with soft-boiled eggs and labne 200

F

fajitas, beef 95
falafel with eggplant puree and tomato salsa 184
frittata
    bacon, leek and potato 119
    hot smoked salmon and goat's cheese 152
    three-cheese pasta frittata 203
    wild mushroom and green onion 181

G

garlicky beans with pine nuts 225
green bean and tomato salad with hazelnut dressing 232
green mango and coconut salad 148

H

ham, see pork
hoisin and lemon chicken skewers 41
horseradish mascarpone 81

K

koftas, turkey 34
korma curry meatballs 52
korma prawn curry 166
kumara potato jackets 182

L

lamb
  cardamom lamb pilaf with cashew and coriander yogurt 55
  cutlets with pesto baby gnocchi 62
  farfalle 62
  greek lamb meatballs with tomato and mint salad 56
  grilled lamb salad 59
  korma curry meatballs 52
  lamb and black bean stir-fry with sambal 52
  lamb and eggplant pies 60
  lamb and harissa yogurt wraps 70
  lamb fillet salad with green pesto dressing 48
  mint and honey lamb skewers with tzatziki 47
  minty lamb burgers 67
  moroccan lamb cutlets with roasted capsicum couscous salad 51
  spicy lamb salad 67
  spicy pasta with lamb, anchovies and rosemary 68
  spring grilled lamb and warm pea salad 70
  turkish bread with lamb and eggplant 64
lentils
  curried vegetable and lentil soup 190
  pork steaks with sautéed lentils 116
  spiced 220

M

macaroni, tuna 162

mash
  celeriac 215
  fennel 219
  fetta and black olive 217
  kumara 218
  parsnip 216
  pea 214
  pumpkin 218
  roasted capsicum 219
  spinach 215
  wasabi 217
meatballs
  greek lamb meatballs with tomato and mint salad 56
  korma curry 52
  pork and rosemary meatballs with pasta 106
  spanish spicy pork and veal meatballs 123
mushrooms
  chicken, fetta and mushroom pasta 33
  creamy beef and mushroom rigatoni 89
  mixed mushrooms on creamy polenta 186
  mushroom, potato and spinach tortilla 194
  wild mushroom and green onion frittata 181
mussels
  asian 151
  tarragon 161

O

oak leaf and mixed herb salad with dijon vinaigrette 232
omelette, blue cheese and salami 125
orange and maple-glazed baby carrots 223

P

pasta
  cauliflower and cheese pasta bake 181
  chicken, fetta and mushroom 33
  chorizo, tomato and rocket pasta salad 137
  creamy beef and mushroom rigatoni 89
  creamy prawn and tomato spaghetti 144
  curly fettuccine with smoked salmon 158
  lamb farfalle 62
  pork and rosemary meatballs with 106
  pork stroganoff with parsley fettuccine 120
  ricotta and sausage 115
  ricotta and spinach agnolotti 190
  spaghetti with artichokes, asparagus and peas 178
  spicy pasta with lamb, anchovies and rosemary 68
  three-cheese pasta frittata 203
  tuna macaroni 162
pea
  couscous salad with mixed peas and beans 212
  pea, ham and mint soup 113
  peas with mint butter 221
  puree 22
  rice and peas 213
  spaghetti with artichokes, asparagus and peas 178
  spring grilled lamb and warm pea salad 70
pesto, cheesy polenta 206
pies
  lamb and eggplant 60
  salmon 151
pilaf 212
  cardamom lamb pilaf with cashew and coriander yogurt 55
  indian chicken 41
  turkey 21
pizzas, taleggio, prosciutto and rocket 110
polenta
  cheesy pesto 206
  mixed mushrooms on creamy polenta 186
  soft 206
pork, see also chorizo; prosciutto
  blue cheese and salami omelette 125
  chinese pork and noodle soup 133
  chops with blue-cheese sauce and cauliflower mash 130
  cutlets with baked parsnips and apples 109
  grilled miso pork cutlets 134
  pea, ham and mint soup 113
  pork and brussels sprout stir-fry 126
  pork and mango curry 125
  pork and rosemary meatballs with pasta 106
  pork, orange and coriander salad 113
  puttanesca potato bake 119
  ricotta and sausage pasta 115
  sausages with crispy potatoes and cabbage 129
  spanish spicy pork and veal meatballs 123
  steaks with sautéed lentils 116
  stroganoff with parsley fettuccine 120
  sweet and sticky ginger pork cutlets 109
  thai chilli pork 134
potato see also mash
  bacon, leek and potato frittata 119
  chicken and potato salad 38
  lyonnaise potatoes 231

index 239

mushroom, potato and spinach tortilla 194
the perfect rösti 228
pork sausages with crispy potatoes and cabbage 129
potato puree 216
potato salad with herbed cream 230
puttanesca potato bake 119
salmon and potato parcels 140
sautéed potatoes 230
warm potato and smoked trout salad 166

prosciutto
   baked witlof with 129
   prosciutto-wrapped bean bundles 224
   prosciutto-wrapped cutlets with truss tomatoes 77
   taleggio, prosciutto and rocket pizzas 110

pumpkin
   curried pumpkin crêpes 199
   jerk chicken with pumpkin and onion 14
   roast pumpkin and chickpea salad 186

puttanesca potato bake 119

R

rice
   pilaf 212
   rice and peas 213
   steamed ginger 214
   yellow coconut 213

ricotta and sausage pasta 115
ricotta and spinach agnolotti 190

S

salad
   baby spinach and parmesan 233
   beef and mixed sprout 78
   caprese 207
   char-grilled thai squid 156
   chicken and potato 38
   chorizo, tomato and rocket pasta 137
   coleslaw 233
   couscous salad with mixed peas and beans 212
   crisp parmesan chicken with eggplant 14
   fennel, cabbage and radish 173
   green bean and tomato salad with hazelnut dressing 232
   green mango and coconut 148
   grilled lamb 59
   lamb fillet salad with green pesto dressing 48
   lemon and thyme veal cutlets with beetroot salad 82
   lime and coconut snake bean 226
   mixed bean salad with hazelnut butter 225
   moroccan lamb cutlets with roasted capsicum couscous salad 51
   niçoise 147
   oak leaf and mixed herb salad with dijon vinaigrette 232
   pork, orange and coriander 113
   potato salad with herbed cream 230
   prawn caesar 158
   roast pumpkin and chickpea 186
   salmon with nam jim on cucumber 165
   spicy lamb 67
   spring grilled lamb and warm pea salad 70
   thai chicken, papaya and peanut 19
   tomato and herb 231
   tomato and mint 56
   vietnamese beef 91
   vietnamese chicken and mango 10
   warm potato and smoked trout 166
   warm roast beef and vegetable 96

salmon, see seafood

seafood
   asian mussels 151
   baked snapper 161
   barbecued chilli prawns with green mango and coconut salad 148
   char-grilled thai squid salad 156
   creamy prawn and tomato spaghetti 144
   crispy parmesan fish fillets 174
   curly fettuccine with smoked salmon 158
   fish chowder with garlic and chive rolls 169
   hot and sour prawn noodle soup 170
   hot smoked salmon and goat's cheese frittata 152
   korma prawn curry 166
   niçoise salad 147
   prawn caesar salad 158
   prawn club sandwich with chips 144
   salmon and potato parcels 140
   salmon patties with fennel salad 173
   salmon pies 151
   salmon with nam jim on cucumber salad 165
   sesame prawn and scallop stir-fry 143
   smoky prawn and chorizo stew 155
   tarragon mussels 161
   tuna macaroni 162
   warm potato and smoked trout salad 166

skewers
   hoisin and lemon chicken 41
   mint and honey lamb skewers with tzatziki 47

soup
   bean and basil 197
   chinese pork and noodle 133
   curried vegetable and lentil 190
   hot and sour prawn noodle 170
   pea, ham and mint 113
   root vegetable soup with cheesy brioche toasts 193
   white minestrone 182

spinach
   baby spinach and parmesan salad 233
   creamed spinach 223
   mushroom, potato and spinach tortilla 194
   ricotta and spinach agnolotti 190

stir-fry
   lamb and black bean stir-fry with sambal 52
   pork and brussels sprout 126
   sesame prawn and scallop stir-fry 143
   sichuan beef 86
   spicy tofu 197
   thai spicy beef and noodle 99

T

tomatoes
   chorizo, tomato and rocket pasta salad 137
   creamy prawn and tomato spaghetti 144
   falafel with eggplant puree and tomato salsa 184
   green bean and tomato salad with hazelnut dressing 232
   prosciutto-wrapped cutlets with truss tomatoes 77
   tomato and herb salad 231
   tomato and mint salad 56

tortilla, mushroom, potato and spinach 194
turkey koftas 34
turkey pilaf 21

V

veal
   lemon and thyme veal cutlets with beetroot salad 82
   prosciutto-wrapped cutlets with truss tomatoes 77
   spanish spicy pork and veal meatballs 123

vinaigrette, preserved lemon 186

W

white bean puree 220
white minestrone 182
wild mushroom and green onion frittata 181
witlof, baked, with prosciutto 129